Peter Reynolds

Practical Approaches to Teaching Shakespeare

Oxford University Press

Oxford University Press, Walton Street, Oxford OX2 6DP

Oxford New York Toronto
Delhi Bombay Calcutta Madras Karachi
Petaling Jaya Singapore Hong Kong Tokyo
Nairobi Dar es Salaam Cape Town
Melbourne Auckland
and associated companies in
Berlin Ibadan

Oxford is a trade mark of Oxford University Press

© Oxford University Press 1991
First published 1991
Reprinted 1992

ISBN 0 19 831954 1

Typeset by Trintype Ltd.,Wellingborough
Printed in Great Britain at the Alden Press, Oxford

To Rex Gibson

Acknowledgements

I am grateful to Jonathan Morris, Head of English at Redwell Comprehensive,
South Shields, Malcolm Wallis, formerly Head of English at Sharnbrook Upper
School, Bedfordshire, and Bernadette Fitzgerald, formerly of Hengrove
Comprehensive School, Bishopston, who read the manuscript of this book; I owe a
good deal to their experience of practical approaches to teaching Shakespeare.
Anyone familiar with the work of Cicely Berry will immediately recognize the debt
that I owe to her. She introduced me to choric speech as a way of approaching
Shakespeare. I have also learnt a lot about how to teach practical drama from the
work of Maggie Pittard, Principal Lecturer in drama at the Roehampton Institute.
As always, the editorial tact and skill of Kimberley Reynolds was invaluable to me.
My debt to the many teachers with whom I was lucky enough to work on the
'Shakespeare and Schools' project of the Cambridge Institute of Education is great.
To them, and especially to the project director – Rex Gibson – this book is
dedicated.

Contents

Introduction

Shakespeare and the National Curriculum

Many teachers believe that Shakespeare's work conveys universal values, and that his language expresses rich and subtle meanings beyond that of any other English writer. Other teachers point out that evaluations of Shakespeare have varied from one historical period to the next, and they argue that pupils should be encouraged to think critically about his status in the canon. But almost everyone agrees that his work should be represented in a National Curriculum. Shakespeare's plays are so rich that in every age they can produce fresh meanings and even those who deny his universality agree on his cultural importance. The Shakespeare and Schools project, at the Cambridge Institute of Education, has shown that secondary pupils of a wide range of abilities can find Shakespeare accessible, meaningful and enjoyable. The project has demonstrated that the once-traditional method where desk-bound pupils read the text has been advantageously replaced by exciting, enjoyable approaches that are social, imaginative and physical. This can also be achieved by: use of film and video recordings, visits to live theatre performances, participation in songs and dances, dramatic improvisations, activities in which Shakespeare's language is used by pupils interacting with each other. Pupils exposed to this type of participatory, exploratory approach to literature can acquire a firm foundation to proceed to more formal literary responses should they subsequently choose to do so.

English for ages 5 to 16, Chapter 7, paragraph 16, June 1989.

This paragraph from the Cox Report on the development of English in the National Curriculum clearly illustrates both the importance given to Shakespeare, and the enthusiasm of the report's authors for recent developments in practical approaches to teaching the plays. The question for those in schools charged with carrying out the guidelines eventually issued by the Secretary of State for Education is *how* to plan and execute an approach to teaching Shakespeare that is more than 'desk-bound', and which is also an 'exciting, enjoyable' experience. All teachers naturally want their work to be exciting and enjoyable both for themselves and for their pupils, and many will justifiably respond to Cox by saying that so-called 'desk-bound' work *can* be exciting and enjoyable if it is well taught.

Whatever the arguments may be concerning the merits of traditional vs non-traditional approaches to teaching Shakespeare, this book addresses the question of how best to construct a teaching strategy that is not desk-bound, but is 'social, imaginative and physical'. That strategy involves work requiring the full and active participation of *all* pupils, for, as Cox and his colleagues rightly emphasize, whatever the merits of more traditional methods of teaching, there is also a need for an approach that is 'active and investigative, rather than passive and prescribed' (8.17). The practical approaches to teaching Shakespeare that are set out here are open to any competent teacher of English; they require no specialist knowledge of, or training in, drama. Not only is this a practical approach, I hope too that it is a *practical* book.

The Shakespeare paradox

The guests on BBC Radio 4's *Desert Island Discs* are always asked to choose, in addition to their eight records, a luxury item and a book. However, as regular listeners will know, the book cannot be either the Bible or the works of Shakespeare as these are already on the island. It is not just the bracketing together of the book that forms the basis of one of the world's great religions with the work of a long dead Elizabethan playwright that is striking, but the explicit assumption that all the cast-aways would *want* the works of Shakespeare on their island with them. It is an extraordinary feature of Britain in the late twentieth century that, although relatively few of its population would claim regularly or even occasionally to see the plays of Shakespeare in performance, and even fewer would say that they read him for pleasure, his name and reputation bestride our culture like a colossus.

Perhaps nowhere is the Shakespeare paradox more clearly visible than in the televised version of the children's classic, *Batman*. It is a bust of the Bard, standing on a table in the book-lined study of millionaire Bruce Wayne which conceals the switch that gives access to the Bat Poles and the Bat Cave. The assumption is that the young viewers of this popular programme (most of whom will never have seen or read a single Shakespeare play) will identify the playwright and associate Wayne (Batman) and his nephew (Robin) with a life of refinement and culture. This epitomizes the power and peculiar nature of the Shakespeare paradox.

In Britain an ability to demonstrate a knowledge of Shakespeare opens access to a great deal more than the 'Bat cave'. The name 'Shakespeare' has become a part of the fabric of contemporary British society.

Shakespeare as a commercial logo is readily understood. His image has been used to lend dignity and status to everything from £20 pound notes to beer and cigars. The theatre company that bears his name, was, until very recently, the only one accorded 'Royal' status. To work for it, or to be associated with it, confers kudos. Anyone remotely interested in the theatre knows that almost all of those distinguished actors whose names have appeared in the honours list (Lord Olivier, Sir John Gielgud, Dame Peggy Ashcroft and, most recently, Dame Judi Dench) all made their reputations as classical actors and, in particular, as players of Shakespeare.

The Bard himself may be long dead, but a monument to his name exists, a monument whose growth seems inexhaustible in scale and reputation. To some it is a living monument, serving as an inspiration. But to others, and especially to the academically less able, the edifice can have a deadening effect, engendering a potent cocktail of responses ranging from awe and respect, to fear and dread. Neither is particularly helpful to constructive thought. From fear usually arises dismissal: Shakespeare's boring, irrelevant, etc. Awe generates an almost equally negative response which automatically assumes that everything the man once wrote is above criticism: his work is, like holy writ to a fundamentalist believer, perfect, 'unique', 'for all time' etc.

GCSE

Until quite recently, Shakespeare's position at the core of the English curriculum has been unchallenged. His plays have been studied, celebrated, and performed by generations of students. However, in the face of growing apathy and overt hostility from significant numbers of school students, there has been a noticeable withdrawal of support within some state schools from the very idea of trying to teach Shakespeare at all, and certainly to question the wisdom of attempting to introduce his work earlier in the curriculum, and to non-examination students. It remains to be seen what practical effect the recommendations of the Cox report will have in schools, but the advent of GCSE has for the first time given teachers the power to opt out of studying Shakespeare in public examinations. How many teachers, or perhaps more to the point, how many heads of departments of English in secondary schools, will avail themselves of this new opportunity remains to be seen. On the other hand, GCSE, especially Mode 3 schemes, could be seen by some teachers as the potential salvation of the teaching of Shakespeare in schools.

GCSE may allow teachers to opt out, but for those who opt in it offers enormous scope to teach the text exactly as they wish. But, there remains a real possibility that hopes for an increasing and enthusiastic commitment to teaching Shakespeare at *all* levels will be lost in parts of the state system unless the enthusiasm of teachers for teaching Shakespeare can be re-kindled.

One of the objectives of this book is to help to counter that possibility by suggesting practical ways of involving young people of widely differing abilities and ages in the process of re-claiming Shakespeare for themselves. If Shakespeare's works are not to become even more divisive indicators of class, education and culture, the undergrowth surrounding them has to be cleared. Shakespeare studies can, and I feel should, continue to play a lively part in a changing curriculum. They can usefully be accommodated to new examination procedures for, as critics have long established, the plays can be read in conjunction with other works to enhance understanding of developments in literary studies. Not only can the language and ideas of the plays inspire and uplift the imagination and intellects of young and old alike, but they are valuable for the potential way in which they can involve the young in an examination of relevant issues and ideas.

If this potential is to be fully realised for *all* students, not simply a minority, it is essential that teachers use the opportunity presented by GCSE and 'open text' GCE 'A' level exams to review their practice of teaching Shakespeare. They must resist the temptation to placate initial hostility by avoiding Shakespeare in favour of more 'relevant' material. I hope that the exercises and general approach outlined in this book will encourage them to confront the problems of teaching Shakespeare at *all* levels through a dynamic pedagogical strategy that involves all the students equally in a collective and collaborative enterprise. The basis of that strategy is a practical approach.

Starting Shakespeare

Traditionally many schools have always left starting Shakespeare until pupils reach the upper school and are embarking upon the preparation for public examinations. However, there are increasingly large numbers of teachers who advocate pushing the experience much lower down the age range; indeed, I have seen some of the most innovative and success-ful Shakespeare teaching taking place in Junior schools. My own practical approach to teaching Shakespeare applies to a broad range of both age and ability. As the reader will see, most of the exercises outlined in Chapters 2 (p. 30) and 3 (p. 67) of this book could be adapted for use by those starting out on Shakespeare studies for the first time. Most of the material on *A Midsummer Night's Dream* could certainly be used in the first school, with children aged from 7–11.

The problem of language

I first began thinking seriously about practical approaches to teaching Shakespeare when I encountered the difficulties experienced by intelligent undergraduates when asked to read aloud the text of a Shakespeare play. Their painful stumbling progress very often managed only to mutilate the meaning of the text, and to alienate the attention of the rest of the listeners. Indeed, the main barrier constantly cited by students of all ages (as well as their teachers) that initially prevents them from coming to terms with Shakespeare is not the range or complexity of the ideas, the philosophy, or historical context, but the language of the late-sixteenth century. Reading it is difficult, speaking it aloud seemingly impossible and best left to professionals (or, in their absence too often, the teacher).

I began to think of ways in which the combination of embarrassment, humiliation, and boredom suffered by generations of young people when asked to read Shakespeare aloud in class could be avoided.

Why a *practical* approach?

I should say that many of the techniques used here were first developed for teaching drama. Indeed, my first experience of a basic choric approach to Shakespeare came from watching and listening to Cicely Berry at the RSC. However, in writing this book, what I am interested in is not drama as a subject in its own right (although of course it is this), but in de-mystifying the use of drama as a teaching technique applied to Shakespeare.

I hope the ideas I outline here will appeal to all teachers who have a lively and open approach to their work and can potentially therefore make excellent use of dramatic techniques to enhance their teaching, and thus the learning experience of their students. But this is not a book about putting on plays, or about getting young people to 'act'. Nor is the use of a practical approach to Shakespeare intended to be a replacement for more formal 'desk-bound' modes of study. It is an additional input, designed for use by English teachers, as well as their drama colleagues, to stimulate thought through a lively engagement of both intellect and emotion.

Working practically is particularly useful for overcoming students' awe and alienation when they encounter Shakespeare. It helps the teacher break free from the force-feeding, teacher-centred situation which is unproductive because one-way. This practical approach is *process* and not *product* orientated. It is designed to be enjoyable, and I hope it is also exciting, but at the same time its real purpose is to encourage the participants to 'think on their feet'. There are no 'starring' roles; all the group participate on an equal basis. No elaborate properties or costumes are required, a 'stage' is absolutely unwanted. There are few rules other than:

> There are no spectators.
> The work of individuals, as opposed to that of the group,
>   is never exposed unless positively requested.
> Everyone has an equal share of the activity.
> Responsibility for the success or failure of a session
>   is *shared* between students and their teacher.

The work requires no specialist drama skills, but precisely the same qualities as any good teaching: thorough preparation, a willingness to take calculated risks, and an open mind.

Practical work essentially involves creating a context in which the language of the play is to be spoken. Creating that context requires from the students a combination of intellectual, physical, and emotional activity. It is therefore an opportunity for students to direct their natural energy into positive channels. Instead of sitting behind a desk, they are able to move, and encouraged to speak and interact with one another. The exercises are designed to keep everyone actively and productively engaged. For instance, the section on *choric speech* (Chapter 2, p. 30) describes how speeches assigned in the text to one character can be broken down and shared by a whole group. No participant speaks more than another; the 'meaning' is constructed communally. Music and action may be added as part of what is essentially a game which helps make archaic language familiar, and constructs a picture of, for instance, relationships inscribed within the play as a whole.

As part of the recent Leverhulme-funded research project, Shakespeare and Schools, I have had the opportunity to work with teachers and also school students currently engaged in studying Shakespeare for assessment. I found that many of the practical techniques used by actors studying Shakespearean texts which had proved useful in my work with undergraduates could easily be modified for the classroom. Indeed, many actors have recently been rushing into print talking about their way of approaching Shakespeare, and in the section on further reading at the end of this book I draw attention to some titles that have proved useful in my own teaching.

In my experience what actors say about what they do in playing Shakespeare can sometimes prove to be very helpful, not necessarily as a substitute to traditional 'lit crit', but as a way of enlarging one's perspective on the text as a whole. Although you may not want or expect your students to read Antony Sher talking about his preparation for playing the leading role in *Richard III* (in *Year of the King*), or to hear five distinguished performers discussing playing the leading female roles in *As You Like It, Macbeth, Measure for Measure, The Taming of the Shrew, All's Well That Ends Well,* and *Cymbeline* (in Carol Rutter's *Clamorous Voices: Shakespeare's Women Today*), you may find it invaluable.

Some teachers, whose training included work in drama, will find parts of this book, such as the introductory games on p. 16, familiar territory. However, there will be many more, perhaps especially teachers of English, who feel insecure about a practical approach to teaching their subject. That insecurity stems from a lack of knowledge or experience of what practical work can contribute to teaching and learning, and also to a very real fear that, once out of the familiar surroundings of the classroom and into the open spaces of the hall or drama studio, chaos will ensue. But pandemonium does not necessarily break out when students get their feet out from under their desks.

Control is always a potential problem for any teacher faced with a lively group of adolescents. In Chapter 1 (p. 16), I discuss strategies for coping with it. But, unlike the classroom, where for the most part the learning is too often entirely teacher-centred, in practical work the responsibility for learning is more evenly shared amongst the class as a whole. It will not happen at once, but, in my experience, as the class gradually becomes aware of what it is achieving, students will become much more self-disciplined and cooperative. They begin to control themselves. I have used this practical approach with groups ranging in size from 8 to 40, and in age from 12 to 65. Teachers with whom I have worked on INSET courses and who have subsequently experimented with these techniques in their own teaching have also found that the response of the students is overwhelmingly positive. They enjoy the sense of power and control that comes from animating words that, on the printed page, had seemed flat and remote. The students enjoy owning Shakespeare's language in a practical session whether it be a word, phrase or line.

What a practical approach involves

At its simplest, it is a fact that any attempt to vocalise the words that Shakespeare wrote begins to transform them by the addition of the speaker's own consciousness or instinctive interpretation: we complete the text by the act of reading it. There is no neutral way of speaking a text (or of hearing the words spoken in the theatre in the mind). When Hamlet says 'To be or not to be, that is the question', what it means depends on the dramatic context in which it is heard, and not least on what the actor speaking the lines conveys to an audience that it means to *him* at any given moment.

One of the aims of the practical approach to Shakespeare outlined in this book is to encourage students to explore the vast range of possibilities for meanings that become apparent once the spoken text begins to be directly experienced in a dramatic context. For example, selected passages can be subjected to experiments involving different ways of stressing selective words or phrases, or by what happens when a pause is inserted in a line. For example, in the Rosalind-Orlando wooing scene from *As You Like It* (IV.1) Rosalind (disguised as Ganymede) asks the young and love-sick Orlando 'how long you would have her after you have possessed her?' If the actor stresses the first 'have' and inserts a brief pause after the second, it gives an emphasis to 'possessed' and indicates a Rosalind speculating on the inevitable sexual conclusion to this ritual courtship.

As well as being able to explore the use of emphasis and pause, practical exploration of a play (especially of the kind outlined in Chapter 4 P. 96) can demonstrate a fundamental element which is too often neglected in literary study of Shakespeare. That is that Shakespeare's language is rhetorical. When an actor speaks what a dramatist has written, unless it is in soliloquy, there will almost invariably be other actors who are listening to what is said, and in performance listening is an expressive act. The audience, of course, also participate in this process for *everything* said on stage is intended to be heard by them. This un-spoken text is a vital ingredient in the manufacture of meanings. Indeed, the actor speaking enacts one text; the actor(s) listening en-acts another, but *the* text belongs not to the actors, but to the audience who watch the inter-action of the players and make their own sense (text) out of it.

I hope, as your students gain confidence, they will see that, through an active involvement in practical Shakespeare teaching, *they,* as well as their teachers, are actively engaged in manufacturing meanings and are excited by this. These meanings are significant, and worthy of consideration. The student who participates in collaborative dramatic exploration of Shakespeare is creating an opportunity to stake a claim to that text that is personal, and not simply that of their teacher.

Finally I have stressed the value to students of a collaborative approach to learning. That collaboration can of course extend to teachers. Why not discuss some of the ideas in this book with a colleague and agree to work together on some sessions? It can be liberating as well as useful not only to have some moral support, but also another person to take part with you, and help monitor the progress of the session. You could perhaps agree beforehand that both of you will be jointly responsible for the planning of the session, and that you will alternate directing and participating in the class.

The colleague does not of course have to be a teacher of English. In my work for the Shakespeare and Schools project, I learnt of a school in Cambridgeshire where staff collaborated to allow fourth year pupils to devote a whole term to work derived from *The Tempest*. All their English, Humanities, Art, Music, and even some Science was derived in some way from the text.

Whether or not you work with others or on your own, I hope that this practical approach to teaching Shakespeare will be enjoyable, and that you will come to see it as a valuable weapon in the continuing struggle to open up the excitement and joy of studying Shakespeare to students of all ages and abilities.

1

Rites of Transition

The first thing to remember when planning a practical session on Shakespeare is that what takes place is not meant to *substitute* for more traditional methods of work, but to *complement* them. In the introduction I outlined some of the more obvious reasons why young people are often reluctant to sit down, read, and subsequently discuss a play by Shakespeare. Each of the sections which follow in this chapter is designed to break down barriers and facilitate discussion and understanding. The goal of each practical workshop is to provoke a lively communal discussion of Shakespeare's text to which *all* the members of the group feel able to contribute. After a practical exercise, everyone has participated in speaking a text; as a consequence it is not necessarily the more articulate, traditionally academic members of the group who dominate the closing discussion.

The practical method outlined in this chapter (and in the book as a whole) has the advantage of being easily adapted for different age and ability levels and for groups of different size. Indeed, the 'choric' approach outlined at the end of this chapter and developed in detail in chapters 2 (p. 30) and 3 (p. 67), can be used at almost *any* level of ability: from those starting Shakespeare in the Primary school, through GCSE to 'A' level and undergraduate students. Once the basic *method* is grasped the limits of its application are defined only by the imagination and skill of the teacher using it.

Organizing a practical session

Try to keep the mood of all practical sessions as relaxed and informal as you can: this will encourage the responsiveness of the group. Whenever you finish an exercise on a text in which everybody has participated actively, always sit down in a circle with the students to discuss it. Sit on the floor, don't use chairs.

The students and you should wear soft shoes (or no shoes at all) and preferably clothing that does not restrict movement. They need to be warned not to wear their best clothes. If you work in a school in which the students wear a uniform, consider asking them to bring jeans and T-shirts for practical sessions. I know that this will not always be practicable, and it certainly isn't worth the trouble for a 35 minute session based in a classroom. But in my experience for anything longer it *really* helps in signalling the change to the new style of the work.

A practical session works best when organized in two distinct phases. The first is primarily concerned with making the group cohesive and establishing an atmosphere of confidence, cooperation and concentration. This is done by using a series of exercises and 'games'. This stage is very important and must not be rushed through in order to get onto the 'real' work of speaking Shakespeare's text. Encourage your students to think of this time as a kind of mental 'air lock' which they have to pass through in order to signal the difference in expectation and role from those usually adopted in more conventional modes of teaching and learning.

The second stage is focused on the text by first speaking it and then discussing it. But, unlike 'reading round the class', students are not asked to master or analyse lengthy and complex passages of text. Instead the text is previously broken down by the teacher into discrete and easily manageable units which are then reconstructed by the group as a whole through a series of exercises and more games. Unlike classroom readings, these will not expose individual weakness, consequently the participants are excited rather than daunted by the language. Any reading of a line produced individually or collectively is valid and useful during these exercises, but as the students come together and reassemble a given passage, interesting interpretative work takes place almost unconsciously. This is the greatest advantage of working in this way with reluctant as well as with keen and enthusiastic students. It doesn't feel like learning; the thinking processes are all part of the games, which enable the student to possess his or her lines in a way which is entirely unlike the usual reading experience.

One of the most difficult things about starting practical work for the first time (and indeed subsequently) is the inevitable degree of excitement and apprehension it generates among the students and the potential problems of control that are therefore raised. It is, for many of them, quite a novelty to be beginning an English lesson not behind a desk with a text in front of them, but on their feet without a text in sight. It is also likely to be for them (as it is for you) a situation in which they feel insecure and unsure of what is expected of them. Usually this insecurity manifests itself in laughter and general high spirits. Some, often the most academically bright amongst them, will immediately say (or think to themselves), 'What on earth has this got to do with studying Shakespeare? Will it get me through my exams?' Others may see it as a glorious opportunity to have fun at your expense. So, from the moment the students enter the room keep them active.

Introductory games and physical exercises

Preparation

To make a practical session work takes confidence and careful monitoring of time and conditions. It also requires, especially in the early stages, thorough preparation. Indeed, the value of carefully selecting and then deconstructing text for students to subsequently reconstruct cannot be overstressed: it is the heart of this practical approach. But, once the preparation has been done, the work can be re-used again and again.

1 Select a Shakespeare sonnet and break it up into manageable sections for subsequent distribution amongst the group as a whole. (See p. 24 for an example.)

2 Bring a cassette tape recorder or record player (one that produces a good volume of sound) and one or two music tapes or records. (See below for suggestions.)

3 Try to book a large space (the hall or gym would be ideal) which is suitable for the exercises you have prepared. (If this is not possible, the classroom will do.)

Timing

Most teachers are more likely to be constrained in what they can achieve by the demands of the timetable rather than their ability to make effective use of this practical approach. Most will have little more than 70 minutes, some as little as 35 per session to complete the exercises and the discussions. In the following guidelines for running practical workshops I have provided a variety of exercises and *suggested* the approximate amount of time each should take. So much depends on individual factors such as the size, character, and mood of a group, their degree of familiarity with practical work etc, that it is impossible to be precise about the time needed to complete an exercise. Obviously an approach which is relatively new to you (and to your students) is likely to take up more time than one already familiar. Therefore as a general rule, when starting out on a practical approach, do try, if possible, to arrange for one or two double sessions of at least 60-70 minutes each.

The work described in this chapter, and divided into two phases, should be completed in a session lasting no longer than 70 minutes. However, don't worry if you find yourself short of time and unable to get through the whole session. It is much less important to complete all the exercises than it is, especially in the early stages, to establish an atmosphere of mutual trust. Your primary goal is to generate an awareness in the students of what they are potentially capable of achieving. If a particular exercise seems to be working well stay with it and try out some variations. Similarly, if the group isn't responding, move on and change the tempo.

Preparing the room

I don't assume that every teacher has constant access to the school hall or to other relatively large open spaces. Obviously if you can use such a space when exercises seem to require it you should, but a lot of the practical work outlined in this book can be achieved without moving outside the classroom. For example, all the work in Chapter 4 Walking Through (p. 96) can easily be done there. For most of the exercises in Chapters 2 (p. 30) and 3 (p. 67) it will be necessary to have a reasonably large open space in which to work, or at least to have cleared the centre of a room by pushing back the desks and tables against a wall. But for others students need not move from their seats. Indeed, there are occasions (for instance, when working on soliloquies) when it may be advantageous to use a small confined space. But whatever space you do use, you will need to take some simple steps to prepare it for a practical session.

In the hall or gym

If you are lucky enough to have access to a large space, the first thing to do is make sure that, as far as possible, you close that space off from the rest of the building. Many school halls have large areas of window space looking out onto the grounds or other parts of the building. If you can, have the students draw curtains or blinds as soon as they enter the space. It is important to do this because it helps enormously in getting the group to concentrate and focus their attention on the exercises you are about to start. It also prevents distractions coming from outside and stops any sense of the participants being on display or having to 'act' for the benefit of others.

Being enclosed in this way also creates a sense of privacy and of being 'cut-off' from the rest of the school - an enormous help in creating and sustaining the level of concentration demanded by this work. The final advantage in being able to close off your chosen space from surrounding areas is that you can blackout, or at least reduce the light levels in the room dramatically. As you will see, this can be very useful in helping both concentration and the manufacture of appropriate mood and atmosphere.

Have the students make the maximum open space possible by clearing and stacking chairs that may hinder movement and placing them around the extreme edge of the room. Stack the chairs if possible - you want to avoid anyone sitting on them.

In the classroom

If you are planning to work in the classroom, here too it can be useful to change the appearance of the room and specifically to control the amount of light coming in. Make as much space as possible by having students move chairs to the sides of the room and stacking them. If there is a carpet that might cause people to trip, roll it up. Again, draw the curtains and/or close the blinds. Close all the doors leading into the room.

Using background music

A great help in creating a good working atmosphere and in helping avoid embarrassment is to use recorded music. From the moment the group enters the teaching space I always have a tape playing quietly but audibly in the background. Then, during the majority of the non-vocal exercises, I use recorded music as a background. You will help students and yourself to get over any initial suspicion of practical methods by using music in this way. It really doesn't matter initially what kind of music, but volume acts as a smokescreen and helps cover any sense of embarrassment.

I currently use Paul Simon's *Gracelands* or something by the Bhundu Boys, and I keep it going for at least the first five minutes of the session. Avoid anything too instantly recognisable; it is likely to carry with it too many associations of no immediate use to you. Also the latest chart topping recording, although sure to please, is unlikely to produce anything other than disco-dancing!

After the first five minutes (always the most difficult time for teachers and students alike) when you move on to other games and exercises, keep using music but try to match it to the exercise. For example, in an exercise requiring expressive use of the body try to match that expression by choosing expansive, lively music like Sousa marches or circus music.

In Chapters 2 and 3 I outline a more specific use for music, showing how it can help enormously to create an appropriate mood and atmosphere for speaking Shakespeare. In the Discography (p. 116) you will find suggested a wide range of music which can be used most effectively when teaching Shakespeare. As you will see, the music ranges from Renaissance to contemporary electronic; some of it was inspired by Shakespearean texts, others by circuses, African music, and so on.

Starting practical work

The objectives of this opening sequence are:

1   To introduce the students to practical exercises that make use of their physical resources in a controlled and disciplined manner.

2   To overcome the initial shock of new found freedom in a new space with a new student/teacher relationship and to create a good working atmosphere of mutual trust, concentration, and cooperation.

3   To make maximum effective use of the teaching space.

Whatever you do, whether you are planning to work in a hall or classroom, *don't* let the students come in at the beginning of the session and sit down. Not all of the time spent in these sessions will be spent thinking on the feet, but you will avoid the awkwardness that sometimes accompanies getting up from the relative security provided by a desk and chair by not giving them an opportunity to sit.

It may be that the students already have some experience of practical drama but don't assume that this is so, nor that the experience that they have had will necessarily be helpful in the kind of work you are proposing. Don't spend any time at the beginning of a session trying to explain what it is that you hope to achieve by this new approach. The less you have to say at the outset the better.

Simply inform the group that the objective is to explore Shakespeare practically and that you will allow time at the end of the session for discussion. From then on, what you need to do is to reassure them that you know what you are doing and you can best achieve this by being clear at the outset as to exactly what it is that you want the students to do. You need to run the first few minutes of any session with authority and precision; then, as the work begins to progress and the students become familiar with a new way of working, you can begin to relax and take a less assertive role.

In working through the exercises that follow remember not to isolate any individual and certainly to avoid drawing attention to any one for *whatever* reason. Treat the group as a whole and if you need to speak to an individual to encourage or discourage him or her in any way, try to do it when the rest are occupied doing an exercise. It is important at the start of the work that shy and tentative individuals feel that they can hide behind the anonymity of the group. It is inevitable that many of the students taking part for the first time will assume, despite what you tell them to the contrary, that they are going to have to act Shakespeare. This will lead to a fear of having to act in front of others, and, to those often almost crippled with self-consciousness, the fear of exposure to the ridicule of their peers is real and acute. Such anxieties are usually dissipated through the exercises which follow.

If a practical class is likely to be an unfamiliar activity to most of those taking part, the initial expectations and levels of energy are likely to be high. I suggest therefore that the first thing you do after the room is prepared is to play a game that allows the students to express that energy, but in a controlled way. I usually start my own sessions with one or two games of tag.

Games

All three Tag games need space, and should not be attempted in the classroom. Later in the chapter there are alternative exercises that can be used to achieve the same results in a smaller space. For all the tag games, a 'catch' is signified by a light touch on the body.

Hopping tag

Choose two people to be the catchers. They must touch as many other people as possible, and those caught must sit on the floor. The twist to the game is that all the players can only move about the space on one leg at a time.

Crab tag

Choose three catchers and have everyone move about the space by walking on their feet and hands. Have them sit with their feet in front and hands behind, they lift their bodies off the floor and move using feet and hands ... like a crab. When players are caught they lie down and form an obstacle for the catchers, a defence for the rest.

Group tag

Pick one (fast!) person to be 'It'. Explain that every time someone is caught she or he joins hands with the catcher(s) and together they go after the rest until all are caught.

Tag lets off energy and makes for simple physical contact between the students by holding hands and/or touching. You need to maintain sufficient control to prevent excessive energy from becoming overstimulating to the point of explosion. I find the best aid in these opening games is that old teacher's friend - the loud whistle.

If the space is really too restricted to accommodate 30 or so young people running or hopping, or if you have doubts about the wisdom of starting with such a vigorous activity, then stipulate that all the players (including the catcher) can only move in a restricted way as in Crab tag. The game can be varied (and made more controlled) by having the catcher(s) and players moving on tiptoe, on their heels etc.

In the opening minutes, these and any other exercises taken from books suggested in the recommendations for further reading (p. 119), or devised by yourself, should be planned in order to make maximum use of the whole teaching space, to use the body in different ways and to involve a certain degree of collaboration and cooperation in the group as a whole. However, if you feel that such an expressive exercise might not suit an already boisterous group then Moving mixtures or Creeping up are good alternatives.

Moving mixtures

Have a music tape playing as background sound. Get the students to begin by walking around the space trying to keep at a fixed distance from each other, say 5–10 feet depending on the area available and the numbers participating. Get them to begin by moving at a brisk, but not running, pace. At a signal from you (clapping your hands, blowing your whistle, banging on a cymbal) change direction. Keep them moving, and at another signal from you, change the nature of the movement e.g. backwards, sideways, on the heels, both knees bent, stiff legs, on tiptoe etc. Conclude the game by asking them to invent a novel way of moving around the room.

Creeping up

This game is calmer than the others and involves much more physical control and self-discipline as well as the cooperation of the whole group. This exercise is particularly useful as it uses individuals as well as the group as a whole. It can be done in a classroom where the desks have been pushed back.

1   Blindfold one member of the group and place him or her on a chair.
2   The others form a circle around this figure and sit on the floor.
3   Take an object such as a bunch of keys and place it under the chair.

The object of the game is to remove the keys without the person sitting on the chair being aware that they have gone. He or she must listen carefully for any hint of movement whilst an individual (you stand outside the circle and point to one person to begin) starts to creep towards the keys. If the blindfolded student hears a noise and points in the right direction (at the oncoming person), then you as referee direct the 'thief' to rejoin the circle and indicate another player to try. If a player succeeds in getting the keys and not being 'seen' she or he is then blindfolded and takes over as guardian of the keys.

This game can quickly absorb the attention of the students and requires both concentration and physical control. It is also a very theatrical exercise for it involves the group as a whole as 'audience' and two major players. Of course the game also takes place in total silence! Everyone in the group does not have to be given a turn at trying to steal the keys nor should you use more than three or four players to be blindfolded. However, Creeping up can take up time and if you are short of it there is a quicker alternative that has similar desired results. It is a variation of Chinese Whispers.

Chinese gestures

1 Have the students form into lines of approximately 8/10 each. They should all stand facing in the same direction, and be asked to remain still and quiet whilst a message is passed from the rear of the line to the front. The message will contain no words but will consist of a variety of gestures.

2 Go to the back of the lines and ask only the person(s) on the end to turn and face you.

3 Tell all the group that you are going to show a coded message to the two students last in line, and that their task will be to start the process of relaying the message up the line. There must be *no* talking during the communication.

4 Demonstrate the message to the rear two only once. Don't make the message too complicated. Try something like this:

   a Tap the top of your head three times with your right hand.

   b Tweak your right ear with your left hand.

   c Rub your tummy in a circular fashion three times with your right hand.

   d Bend both knees and then straighten them.

   e Take your weight onto your left leg and slowly raise your right leg to the side and down again.

5 The students who have been observing you then turn around, tap the people in front of them and attempt to pass on the message; and so on until the last person in line is reached.

6 She or he then shows the line as a whole the gesture (or what it has become).

7 You then show all the students what it looked like originally.

This exercise is fun, and it requires good observation and concentration from the group.

A selection of these games, or others of your own devising, together with the preparation of the room should last for about 10-15 minutes. Do try to remember that this is a crucial time, especially for those students whose experience of this type of work is limited. The exercises are designed to break the ice and develop confidence in you and what you are doing with the group. Therefore be sure of the sequence, and always try to *appear* to know *what* you are doing, and *why,* even if at times you lose sight of it. Don't let the pace of the opening drop. To be effective the momentum needs to be continuous. If you have constantly to consult your notes before saying what you want to happen next, the energy will become dispersed and confidence begin to seep away. If you are not used to leading this kind of activity, you will probably make some minor procedural errors but these are not critical provided you have a clear broad picture of your aims and you adopt a positive approach.

Physical exercises

Up to now we have been playing games with the group as a whole. Now we should move to exercises which involve individuals in the expressive use of their bodies. This group of exercises has been designed to give a structure to, and a reason for, the use of the physical resources of the body in a controlled manner. I generally choose basic actor's loosening-up exercises and make a point of continually encouraging or cajoling the class to do them as best they can. As you will see, most if not all of the work does not require an especially large space, and some, such as 'body limbering', can be done in a classroom.

Body limbering

1   Each person finds a space on the floor big enough so that no one will touch anybody else when their arms are outstretched. (At this point you will begin to see how you are progressing. At the beginning, when the group entered the hall or room, in all likelihood most of them kept to the edges of the space and avoided the centre. Now, when you ask them to find a space, look to see whether or not any brave souls are in or near the centre of it.)

2   Shake the hands hard in front of you, keeping the wrists loose.

3   Do the same with the feet (watch out for anyone wearing slip-on shoes).

4   Vigorously shake the feet and the hands simultaneously for 20-30 seconds.

5   Flop forward from the waist and hang down with head just above the floor.

6   Suggest that the spine, now bent, needs to be straightened. Tell the group to imagine that the spine is like a set of building bricks which have carefully to be erected as a tower, one piece on top of another. At a signal from you everyone should slowly and smoothly come up into a standing position, leaving their heads on their chests until the rest of the body is vertical.

7   Finally, ask them to imagine that a thin line of cotton is attached to the very top of their heads and that this is now beginning to pull the head gently up until the whole body is vertical. Once this exercise is completed, repeat it once or twice.

When you have completed this exercise extend it like this:

1   Standing upright with arms loosely at the side, feet with a small gap between them, think of the head as being very lightly balanced on top of the shoulders and able to move smoothly from side to side as if running on oiled ball-bearings.

2   Move the head as smoothly as possible from right to left and back again. Repeat several times.

3   Hunch the shoulders up tightly and hold them like that for a couple of seconds and then let go. Repeat several times.

4   Choose a partner. In each pair, one of the two is to play the part of the student, the other the teacher. The 'students' have then to attempt to relax sufficiently to allow the 'teacher' to lift the shoulders of the student, hold them there, and then let them drop.

5   Encourage them to go on and see if they can lift a fully relaxed arm or foot (whilst their partner lies on the floor). The object of the exercise is to get to the stage where the 'student' allows the 'teacher' some control over his or her body.

Making shapes

Continuing in pairs (if you have an odd number one group of three will work perfectly well), have the students stand up and without being given time to think about it, at a signal from you, go into a series of different shapes by physically combining their bodies.

1   Take up as much space as possible (there must be a point of physical contact between the pair).

2 Make the smallest possible shape.

3 Make a gnarled and twisted shape.

Whilst this activity is going on *do* offer verbal encouragement. Make sure that you move around the space: never stay too long in the same position.

The creature

1 When the students have made the shapes and used the surrounding space, get them to change partners. Tell the new groupings that you want them to use their bodies to make the shape of a creature. The 'creature' must be an imaginary creation, not one based on observation, so tell them to think about being an amoeba, something from Mars etc.

2 While they begin to do this, walk round the space encouraging them and, when you think them ready, tell them to link up with another couple. This can go on until the whole group is combined.

If the exercise is being done with some degree of concentration, get them to add to it by making the sound that they think appropriate to their particular kind of creature. If you are happy with the way that this exercise is progressing, ask each group *briefly* to show the others the results of their labours. This gets them used to the idea of looking at one another's work, for later on showing and sharing will be very useful. However, if you are running short of time, or feel that at this stage the cooperative spirit might be endangered, move on to the next phase of the introductory session: vocal exercises and speaking Shakespeare.

Vocal exercises

'Heavy breathing'

1 Form a circle looking in to the centre.

2 Expel all the air from the body, then breathe in to a count of five.

3 Hold the breath and hunch up the shoulders.

4 Let the shoulders drop.

5   Breathe out steadily - mouths wide open - to a count of ten.

Begin by explaining that the object of the exercise is to control the expulsion of the air, and that it should all be gone only at the moment you reach ten, *not* before.

Repeat this basic exercise until you are satisfied that all or most of the class are attempting to get it right. Now move on to adding sound.

Humming

The objective is now to experiment with *how* sounds are made, and the first sound to be produced is a hum. Explain this and ask that, as the students breathe out keeping their lips together, they should try to get the breath forward in the mouth so as to make their lips tingle.

Repeat the stages of 'heavy breathing' from 1–4. On 5 (breathing out) they should keep their mouths *closed* and hum. Encourage them to 'think the sound forward'.

Do this exercise once or twice until the volume of sound generated seems roughly commensurate with the numbers in the group. It may help concentration and avoid possible embarrassment if, when doing these exercises for the first time, you ask pupils to keep their eyes closed and to concentrate on making the sound and listening to the quality of it.

Now explain that you want them to add a different kind of sound.

Repeat the 'heavy breathing' stages 1–4. Then, on 5 (breathing out), have them humming but, when you reach the count of 3–4, clap your hands and tell the group to open their mouths wide making an 'Ah' sound until you have finished counting to 10.

Your counting in this and the other breathing exercises should be regular and last approximately 15–20 seconds. You can vary the sound: try all the open vowel sounds. Also get your group to alternate between humming with mouths closed and vocalising the vowel sound aloud.

If the group is working well you can break up the circle at this point and get them to do the exercises whilst walking round the room. Depending on the amount of time you have, it is useful to repeat this series of exercises in vocal preparation by getting the group to work in pairs, going over the exercises once again, with one active and one passive partner. At this stage, one acts as student doing the exercises, the other as teacher, listening, giving instructions, encouragement, counting etc.

At this point, *if* time permits, try giving them the following exercise, which uses spoken language

Alphabet improvising

Divide the group into pairs and explain that they have to improvise a conversation. The rules are:

1   The pair are to speak alternately. Once they have decided who is to speak first, she or he must begin a sentence with a word beginning with 'A'.

2   The second speaker must respond with a sentence beginning with the letter 'B', whilst the first speaker prepares to respond with a sentence starting with 'C' and so on until the pair have completed the alphabet.

3   Stress that the improvised exchange doesn't have to make sense, in fact it's far more fun if it doesn't.

You have now successfully completed the rites of transition. You have broken the ice and introduced students to the practical nature of the work. You have also begun to create for them a positive group dynamic in which confidence in using physical and vocal resources has been developed. You, and your students, are now ready to begin work on the ultimate objective of the session: speaking Shakespeare.

Speaking Shakespeare: the choric method

Your work has gradually introduced the group to the expressive but controlled use of their bodies and voices. Now, they are ready to speak Shakespeare using *choric speech.*

The example I have given on the next page is a sonnet which is short and able to be used in its entirety. It is also very easy to see how it can be broken up into discrete segments. Breaking down the text in this way in order subsequently to rebuild it chorically is a crucial part of preparing for a practical session. Of course, the task isn't always as straightforward as in Sonnet 91, but you will quickly learn from experience and knowledge of your students how long or short to make each section. You will also discover the capacity of individuals to retain material in their short-term memories. The obvious rule is not to give too much too quickly.

As confidence and concentration in the choric method grows, you may find yourself able to increase the length of the sections and hence the length of the passage that you can explore. After a relatively short time, a class of 20–30 should be able to give a choric reading of a lengthy soliloquy which will surprise both you and them in its dramatic effectiveness. You can eventually hand over much of the preparation for choric speaking to the members of the group themselves, asking them to divide up a piece of text, not simply by slavishly following the punctuation of modern editors, but using their own sense of what will work. Before the session you should prepare the sonnet; choose one that the students have not studied previously (you want to avoid predetermined ways of speaking or hearing it).

Prepare the material by dividing it up into discrete sections. Don't divide it so that the sense becomes mutilated. For example, if you want to divide the first line of sonnet 91 (as I have done below), the obvious first break comes after the first statement: 'Some glory in their birth', the next after 'some in their skill', and so on. If you have too many or too few students to undertake one sonnet, then it is equally possible to use other material from Shakespeare, but try to choose something that makes sense out of its dramatic context.

At the final stage in your introductory session, you will distribute the sections to the group: one to each person, asking them to try to remember it. Here is Shakespeare's sonnet number 91 broken down by me. Divisions are marked by the symbol //.

> Some glory in their birth//some in their skill//
> Some in their wealth//some in their body's force//
> Some in their garments//though new-fangled ill//
> Some in their hawks and hounds//some in their horse//
> And every humour hath his adjunct pleasure//
> Wherein it finds a joy above the rest//
> But these particulars are not my measure//
> All these I better in one general best//
> Thy love is better than high birth to me//
> Richer than wealth//prouder than garments cost//
> Of more delight than hawks and horses be//
> And having thee//of all men's pride I boast//
> Wretched in this alone//that thou mayest take
> All this away//and me most wretched make.

When each member has been given a segment of text, you will need to play some games to get them used to speaking their words in a variety of ways. This will help them to learn their lines.

1   If you have split the circle during the breathing exercises, bring it back together for the distribution of lines. Make sure that everyone knows the correct sequence by giving each person a number (1-21 in this case) corresponding to his or her segment of text. Do this as quickly as you can. As you give the lines or phrases, say each twice slowly and clearly and get the student to repeat it to you.

2   Each person must find a space on the floor and begin saying the words over and over to themselves. Once the distribution is complete, you can move on. If necessary (for example with a very large group) you can avoid delay and the possibility of disruptive action by allocating the lines prior to your practical class.

3   The students should walk slowly round the room visiting each corner, avoiding contact with each other. They should be saying their line or phrase to themselves under their breath. Encourage them to try to find as many different ways of saying the words as they can. For example: as if pleading, or as if spoken in anger/regret/fear etc.

4   Keep them moving and after a few minutes, clap your hands and tell them to shout the line aloud, all together. You should spring this on them so as to avoid, as far as possible, too much self-consciousness. Then, without stopping the movement, and again together, ask them to try singing the line! Urge them to explore and relish the sound of words. Young people love the magic and excitement of word production and they seem to know instinctively that much of the meaning comes through the senses and not through the intellect. At this stage sound is everything: comprehension will come later.

5   It is important to get the class working on the physical sounds of spoken language. Ask them to concentrate on the vowel sounds by elongating them in an exaggerated way. Then ask them to look at the consonants and explore the sounds that they make. You can vary the pace of the movement . . . very slow and elaborate (like moving in slow-motion) whilst they are elongating the vowels, quick staccato movement to match quick consonants etc.

6   As a conclusion to this stage of the exploration, ask the group to stand still with eyes closed, and to whisper the words.

When they have completed this it is time to begin putting the whole sequence back together.

1   Have the students standing in a circle. Join the circle yourself, making sure that the person speaking the first line is on your immediate right

(giving them all a number helps). Next to her or him should be the one with the second line, then the third, and so on around until the person immediately on your left has the last line of the sonnet.

2   Ask the group to speak the segments in sequence. Stress that this is simply to establish the order in which they speak and to see how much they can remember. In fact, at this point, you will probably begin to hear some interesting vocal emphasis emerging as individuals forget to think about what the words may or may not mean in their efforts to remember them, and where they come in the piece as a whole. You will probably need to repeat this several times and prompt the group from your copy of the text (the *only* copy required).

3   When you are reasonably happy that they all remember their segments and know when to say them, ask the group once more to begin moving around the room keeping separate from one another. Then tell them that they are going to try to put the sonnet back together. To avoid too much self-consciousness about the process get them to break into a jog and, at the clap of your hands, start to speak the lines in sequence. You can get them to run fast (if it is reasonably safe to do so) and shout, to move at a brisk walking pace and use an ordinary speaking voice and so on. Finally, try turning the light level down and asking them to move to the furthest extremities of the room and then to whisper (a sort of large 'stage-whisper' works best). If you are pleased with this, move them into the centre of the room, and, still keeping the light level down, stand in a tight circle back-to-back and once again whisper the lines or phrases of the sonnet in the correct sequence.

This activity should have produced, at the very least, a far more expressive reading of this sonnet than an individual might have managed had she or he been asked to read it aloud in class.

Follow-up work

The practical work in this introductory session has now come to an end. Using the enthusiasm and momentum it has generated, sit down with the group in a circle on the floor and discuss with them what they think and feel about the text. Don't use chairs, you want to continue the informal and relaxed mood of the session into this, its final, stage. The subsequent discussion is what everything else has been a preparation for: the practical work is not designed as an end in itself but as a process that will stimulate discussion and analysis. *So be sure to leave enough time for it.*

Postscript

It is important, especially in the early stages of practical work, to structure the session in such a way as to allow the group to achieve a particular theatrical objective (in this case the group reading of the sonnet). Once they have experienced for themselves the excitement and sense of achievement that invariably comes when they realize of what they are collectively capable, all your subsequent work on more complex texts will be made easier. If you work towards the manufacture of a theatrical product, and at the end of the session it is generally judged a success, then the initial scepticism that may well have accompanied the early stages will largely have evaporated.

After working practically with a group for some time, you may decide that you can spend less time on warming-up exercises. Indeed, you may feel that they are altogether unnecessary. This is a mistake.

Irrespective of whether or not the students themselves can see the point of doing them, they are invariably valuable as a rite of transition and preparation for working in a different and exacting mode of study. It is most unlikely that you will have the opportunity of working with any group over a sustained period of time. The demands of the timetable means that you are likely to have a maximum of 70 minutes of concentrated time together and then perhaps not see the group again for several days. Whatever you achieve by the end of the session, you cannot expect to pick up from exactly that point when you start again. It is difficult to carry over the successes of one session into the next. Building up confidence and technique is a slow process of one step forward, half a step back. Resist the temptation or the calls of some students, to skip the opening exercises in order to get on with where they left off at the last session. That position is lost and cannot now simply be picked up. You need to be prepared to start again at every session. In this way, the work gradually grows and the students themselves realize that satisfactory and satisfying work comes only as the result of effort and concentration.

Taking on a new way of working always involves a certain amount of risk-taking both on behalf of teacher and student. However well you prepare, and however willing the students, from time to time almost any practical session will break down. It may be due to a variety of reasons, many of which are outside your control: the novelty of this new work may at first be too great for some of them, one or two students will seek to disrupt the others, an exercise you have prepared doesn't work as you hoped and the group as a whole appear deflated and confidence in you ebbs. When this happens, the response can be unruly behaviour which threatens your authority and control. There are one or two simple exercises to introduce at such times. The most useful are those designed to improve the concentration of the students and get them re-focusing on the work. In such instances, before you abandon the session, try these exercises.

1   Have the students seated on the floor, eyes shut. Stress that what you are going to ask them to do is very difficult. Ask them to try hard to empty their minds of all extraneous matter and see in front of them a blank screen. Suggest that the screen is black and onto it will be flashed a series of giant numbers from 1 to 10. The object of the exercise is to see the sequence through from beginning to end without any other image(s) intruding. If the sequence is interrupted by anything other than the projected numbers, then the students must go back again to the blank screen and start again. Use this exercise for 3-4 minutes and, in combination with 2 (below), you will have re-established a mood of concentration and calm and can begin again on more physically demanding practical exercises.

2   Get the students all to lie down on the floor on their backs, well apart from one another, and close their eyes. Ask them to listen first to all the sounds coming from outside the room. Ask them to note in their mind how many sounds they can distinguish and where they originate. Then ask them to switch their focus to the sounds coming from within the room itself.

The greatest enemy of good practical work is poor concentration due to embarrassment and self-consciousness often brought about by the exposure of the individual to a new way of working which isn't immediately recognized as work. In my experience, those most subject to crippling self-consciousness are very often those who are generally regarded as being academically the most able. Their defence mechanism is to dismiss the class session as having little or nothing to do with what they see as academic work. This attitude is most likely to manifest itself during the opening exercises. The only thing you can do is to press on and encourage or cajole the reluctant members of the group. When it comes to the discussion at the close of the session, they will get a chance to contribute in a way in which they find more secure because it is more familiar.

2

Speaking the Text

Whether or not you intend to teach either of the two plays which form the basis for the illustrations to this chapter, I hope you will see that it sets out not only the basic elements common to this practical approach to teaching Shakespeare but also includes many specific exercises that could be used in a practical approach to *any* of his plays. Although the age range for this project work is 14–16, with modifications it could certainly be undertaken by students both older or a good deal younger. I focus below on the representation of magic in *A Midsummer Night's Dream*, however you could as easily decide that your students would be more interested in exploring questions of authority; for example, the ways in which Theseus and Oberon dominate their respective societies. Or you could use similar exercises to explore the tension between the male and female characters, and look at how the mechanicals are both celebrated and ridiculed. The choice is yours.

In the previous chapter we looked at the problems of beginning a practical approach to teaching Shakespeare. The exercises in this chapter based on *A Midsummer Night's Dream* and *Romeo and Juliet*, take us one stage further into more complicated work suitable for those embarking on GCSE. However, some of the exercises on *A Midsummer Night's Dream* have been designed to accommodate very young students including those with no previous knowledge of this, or any other Shakespeare play. Indeed, some of them have been used successfully with primary school children. The chapter will illustrate how choric speech, together with dance, music and the use of masks, can create a theatrical atmosphere designed not simply as an enjoyable experience but also to promote subsequent reflection and discussion and to serve as a stimulus to further written project work.

In this work on *A Midsummer Night's Dream* and *Romeo and Juliet*, as on any other play mentioned in the book, it is not my intention to cover the whole text nor to attempt an overview of its many and complex meanings. As you will already have gathered, working practically is a time-consuming process. Although in my experience young people make highly economic use of whatever time is available, to work from cover to cover in this way would probably take up a greater part of the school year. In any case, these practical workshops are not intended in themselves to teach students everything they need to know about a play in order to pass an examination. They are effective because they make it possible for students to feel *engaged* with the texts, to understand some aspects of their structure and content, and to be interested in making further explorations both in the classroom and independently. In the case of primary school children, the objective is simple: to implant the idea that it is fun speaking Shakespeare and to take with them a positive memory associated with his work. The most basic objective of all this work of speaking Shakespeare is to encourage young people of *all* ages to enjoy Shakespeare's language – to experience it as a pleasurable, sometimes even as a sensual activity and *never* to experience it as threatening. Challenging yes, but not threatening.

A Midsummer Night's Dream

A Midsummer Night's Dream is often chosen by teachers as the introduction to Shakespeare for young people. It is frequently produced in schools and colleges – probably more often than any other play, including those others written by Shakespeare.

These exercises on *A Midsummer Night's Dream* are designed not only to introduce young people to the play and especially to the different kinds of magic that it contains, but also to serve as a first taste of Shakespeare for those in Primary or Middle School and those yet to embark upon the rigours of public examinations. For the latter group especially, the exercises present a structured exploration of the problems raised by the fact that the play is full of supernatural elements of magic. They are designed to encourage questioning about the nature of the world Shakespeare created. They should also help to get a group of potentially sceptical young people to engage with the idea of the possible existence of power for both good and evil in a supernatural, transcendental world. This is important because, even though contemporary scholarship and most professional productions have moved a long way from the high Victorian fascination with the action as an opportunity to present a spectacular evocation of a benign fairy-land, many amateur performances, and certainly most school productions, still display the magical qualities of the wood outside Athens as a sweet, even cloying place. Therefore, in any approach to the play whether reading it for pleasure, for a future examination or with an eye towards performance, it is necessary to resolve the central problem of how to represent magic.

Peter Brook's now legendary production of the play in 1970 succeeded above all else because he managed to find a succession of brilliant theatrical metaphors able to articulate to a sceptical late-twentieth century audience, the magical power of Shakespeare's fairy kingdom.

With primary school children and indeed, with many of those facing up to GCSE for the first time, it is best to assume that none of the group has read or seen the play. While some may have an idea of the plot, this is likely to be fragmentary and predominantly concerned with fairies and asses' heads. This lack of familiarity is not an obstacle to a practical session. In fact, beginning any study of a play with a series of practical workshops is advisable, for what such sessions aim to achieve is a *positive* experience. To be that, it must be a powerful and exciting theatrical exercise, one that is basically fun to do, an alliance of energy and intellect. The work has succeeded if, at the end of each session, the participants have had their curiosity stimulated, their imaginations engaged, and their attention focused on just *some* of the ideas and people that make up the text. At the end of the session they should be left wanting to know more about these people; they should look forward with anticipation both to your next practical session and to more formal discussion of the text in the classroom.

Session 1

Preparation

Read the text carefully, deciding what aspect you wish to explore and making your choices as to which sections are to be spoken by the group.

You will need a good portable cassette tape recorder (with a built-in microphone), recorded tapes, and a blank tape (see the exercises below for details). Listen to the suggestions for music and decide what music you will use.

Before beginning this practical session, devote a conventional session to a discussion of magic and the supernatural. It is not necessary for a group to have read the play at this point: the discussion is concerned with getting them to think about the nature of these qualities so that in workshops and subsequent discussion they can relate what they have thought about to Shakespeare's world. Begin generally and work towards the story of the play.

This opening session is important as it introduces several of the main themes to be explored in the following workshops. While each session deals with different sections and themes from *A Midsummer Night's Dream* they are related by a concern with understanding the nature of Shakespeare's magic world and its relationship to that of the mortals.

1   Ask the class how they first heard about fairies, angels, etc. What did they look like? How were they drawn? Did their parents tell them about the 'tooth fairy'? Was there a fairy at the top of the Christmas tree? If so, why?

2   If the class is of first school children, get them to draw a picture of what they think a fairy looks like.

3   Are there good and bad fairies? With an older group, why not tell them something about the Elizabethan view of the supernatural.

4   Introduce reproductions from paintings that show how people in the past have sought to illustrate the supernatural world. The kind of illustrations would be such things as a postcard of the Tate Gallery's painting by the mad Victorian artist Richard Dadd: *The Fairy Feller's Master Stroke*. (In the bibliography p. 119 there is a short list of paintings inspired by *A Midsummer Night's Dream* and where to see them.)

5   Read the class the story of *A Midsummer Night's Dream* from Bernard Miles' *Five Tales from Shakespeare*, or Leon Garfield's *Shakespeare Stories*. If you can't find either use Lamb's *Tales* or, better still, re-tell it in your own words. Whatever method you choose, it is important from the beginning to stress the dramatic nature of the narrative. The story should be told with as much conviction, emotion and energy as you can muster and never be allowed to become a detached listing of the major events. It doesn't matter in the slightest if all the class are not equally clear about the intricacies of the highly complicated plot. What does matter is that their appetites are whetted for a rich tale of intrigue, of young people rebelling against authority, of falling in and out of love and of supernatural events that are sometimes frightening but always exciting.

Timing

I have divided up the work on both texts into what I hope are manageable time segments. It is very difficult to be precise about the amount of time required for any particular exercise or session: as I have said before, so much depends on the size of the group, the nature of the working space, the level of cooperation etc. On *A Midsummer Night's Dream*, sessions 1–3 can be done in about 35-45 minutes. Session 4 really requires a double period of 70-90 minutes. However, if this is totally impractical, it can be split into two halves of roughly equal length.

Starting practical work

1 Start by using one or two of the warm-up exercises from Chapter 1 (p. 20) or others of your own devising that make expressive use of the body: walking through wet tar, over a very unsafe roof, across a minefield etc. Make full use of the available space and involve the group in cooperative, as well as individually disciplined actions.

2 Get the class moving around the room keeping a distance from one another and whilst they are doing this tell them that you are going to play them some music. Ask them, as they move about at a walking pace, to think about what, if anything, is suggested to them by the sounds they can hear.

3 After 2-3 minutes play a record or tape of music. I suggest music by Vangelis, perhaps something from *Invisible Connections*, but most of his atmospheric music will do equally well.

4 After a few minutes, stop the movement and briefly ask one or two individuals of what the music reminded them. If the response is positive and most want to say something, then let them.

5 Get them moving again, this time using the Vangelis music from the start; if you have had any workable suggestions from the previous exercise, incorporate them in this one. For instance, if someone suggested that the music made him or her think of ghosts, ask them to walk and move like ghosts. In any case, get them to use their bodies expressively in some of the following ways: move as if over broken glass; tar; hot coals; soft spongey turf; a very thin roof which is barely able to support their weight etc.

6 Without stopping the music, ask them now to move as if they were walking in a very thick fog. Tell them to imagine that they have

escaped from a prison and are now being followed. They are desperate to avoid being seen by anybody and moving as if they hoped they were invisible.

7   Sit down on the floor in a circle. The group are going to play a Shakespeare version of Chinese Whispers. Take a phrase or sentence from *A Midsummer Night's Dream* that in some way is connected to magical atmosphere of the forest. Say:

> Now the hungry lion roars,
> And the wolf behowls the moon;
> > *(Puck, V.1 358-359)*

Or:

> We the globe can compass soon,
> Swifter than the wandering moon.
> > *(Oberon, IV.1 97-98)*

Explain that everyone must listen carefully and concentrate hard because the words will only be whispered once and not repeated. Then you begin by whispering the sentence to the person on your immediate right who passes it on to the person on his or her right and so on until finally it reaches you again. When the words make their return, say aloud to the whole group what it was that was last whispered to you. Is there much difference? This simple exercise gets the group listening to something written by Shakespeare as well as having to speak it. If you want, repeat it with a distinctly different piece of text.

The last exercise while similar in some ways to the previous one, is more difficult. Nevertheless, it can certainly be done at *any* level of study.

1   Stand in a circle and say that you are going to start off by clapping your hands once.

2   As soon as you begin, the person on your immediate right also claps, then the person next to him or her and so on round the circle and back to you.

3   Get the group to do this as speedily as they can, passing the sound and the action round and round the circle, trying not to pause even for a split second.

4   Staying in the circle, explain that the group is going to pass a line from the text of the play around, each person speaking one word at a time in the correct sequence. Decide on the line (or part of a

line) – those containing words of only one syllable are good to begin with. For instance:

> If you were men, as men you are in show,
> *(Helena III.2 151)*

5   Say the line together several times.

6   Give the person on your left (don't always begin with the same person) the first word 'If'. The second person takes 'you', the third 'were' and so on until the tenth person ends the line with 'show'. This isn't the end of the exercise. The eleventh person in the circle immediately begins again with 'If' and so on as many times as you like, passing the line round and round the circle.

Try not only to achieve accuracy but also smoothness and clarity. Make it sound as much like one person speaking as possible.

Follow-up work

At the end of the session, sit down with the group in a circle on the floor. Ask them if they enjoyed themselves and encourage any comments on the exercises and on the way you introduced them. Were the instructions clear? What words or images – if any – were striking or puzzling? Finally tell them very briefly the kind of thing you are going to try out in the next practical session.

Session 2

Preparation

1   Bring a tape recorder (or a cassette player with a built-in microphone) into the session. You also need a blank tape.

2   Select some music perhaps from Vangelis or something from Jean Michel Jarre. You will need enough for about ten minutes continuous playing.

3   Go through the text of *A Midsummer Night's Dream* and take out any words or phrases that you think resonate the 'other worldly' quality of the play. For example:

What visions have I seen! *(Titania IV.1 76)*
... enamour'd of an ass. *(Titania IV.1 77)*
... take off this head. *(Oberon IV.1 80)*
... kill'd him sleeping? *(Hermia III.2 70)*
... distracted fear, *(Puck III.2 31)*
My mistress with a monster is in love! *(Puck III.2 6)*
I am a spirit ... *(Titania III.1 149)*
I'll give thee fairies ... *(Titania III.1 152)*
... jewels from the deep, *(Titania III.1 153)*
... a headless bear, *(Puck III.1 106)*
We are haunted! *(Quince III.1 101)*
Night and silence! *(Puck II.2 76)*
I am invisible, *(Oberon II.1 186)*

Starting practical work

Begin the session as usual with 10-15 minutes of introductory exercises and games, making sure that you end with some of those involving the use of the voice (see Chapter 1 p. 20).

Quickly give each person a line from the selection above. As soon as a student has a line, she or he should walk around the space repeating it quietly. Whilst they are doing this, put on the music and ask them to repeat some of the expressive movements from the previous session (e.g. moving as if over broken glass, over frozen snow in bare feet etc.) As they begin to try out these physical movements, ask them to vocalize the words or phrases. They should all speak at once, your task is to move around encouraging them to try speaking in as many different ways as they or you can think of: shouting, whispering, singing, carefully, quickly, very very slowly etc. If some of them are particularly inventive, you could ask them if they will show the others. However, at this stage don't have individuals demonstrating on their own; if some of them do want to show, have them do it in small groups, perhaps 3-4 at a time.

Now set up the tape recorder in the centre of the room. Hold the machine in your arms with the microphone facing away from you. Gather the group as close to you as possible without too much bumping and squeezing! Tell them that you are now going to record their words. Ask for quiet and when you have it, switch on the recording tape. Get the class simply to come up one at a time in any order to within a few inches of the microphone and *whisper* their line into it.

Follow-up work

When they have all done this, sit down in a circle and let them listen to the results. You can experiment with this and repeat it as often as you like . . . it is an absorbing kind of game, and one which involves speaking the lines written by Shakespeare and listening to them intently. When you have a tape that they and you are happy with (i.e. one that uses the sounds of the language expressively) hold onto it. You will be able to use it in a subsequent exercise on the play.

Session 3

Preparation

1   Bring to the session as many different percussion instruments as you can find. If you do not have access to any, you can easily and effectively improvise with combs in paper, empty drink cans for banging on with pencils, empty bottles with different size openings that can be blown across to create sound, sticks that can be rubbed or banged together, etc.

2   Look at Puck's speech from the end of the play (V.1 358-377) beginning 'Now the hungry lion roars' and prepare it for choric speaking as in the previous chapter: (I have divided it into 2 sections – indicated by the mark // – but you may decide to create more or fewer divisions depending on the size of the group.) You may find it helpful and time-saving to write these down and give them out to the group in advance of the class. If you do, write or type the lines clearly, preferably with big print or capitals, on a single piece of paper and then cut it up so that each individual has a copy of his or her line. Tell students to try to remember their particular phrase, but that it is not imperative. In any case they should keep the piece of paper with the lines written on it and bring it to the next practical session. Some people are bound to lose or forget their lines so it is wise to make a photocopy of the original sheet with the lines written or typed on it and bring it to the next practical session yourself. Mark on the sheet the name or initials of the pupil to whom each phrase was given.

3   Make sure before they leave that any person with an unfamiliar word (e.g. Hecate) knows both what it means and how to pronounce it.

Now the hungry lion roars//
And the wolf behowls the moon//
Whilst the heavy ploughman snores//
All with weary task fordone//
Now the wasted brands do glow//
Whilst the screech-owl screeching loud
Puts the wretch that lies in woe//
In remembrance of a shroud//
Now it is the time of night//
That the graves//all gaping wide//
Every one lets forth his sprite//
In the church-way paths to glide//
And we fairies that do run//
By the triple Hecate's team//
From the presence of the sun//
Following darkness like a dream//
Now are frolic//not a mouse
Shall disturb this hallow'd house//
I am sent with broom before//
To sweep the dust behind the door.   *(V.1 358-377)*

Starting practical work

Begin the session with the usual introductory games. By now you will probably have established a pattern based on those you find most successful, but don't become rigid about what you do. Most of all try to relate the opening games to the day's planned exercises. For example, after starting with one of the Tag games followed by some 'heavy breathing' (see Chapter 1 p. 22) try something like this:

1   Have everyone find a space on his or her own, sitting on the floor. Tell them to shut their eyes and imagine a scenario. Give them the following information: you are part of an expedition to a tropical rainforest in South America. The region is wild and totally isolated from civilization. Unfortunately, you have broken your leg and cannot move; the rest of the team have gone off to seek help leaving you alone in your tent. It is night and a steady rain is falling.

Now ask everyone to try, softly at first, to make the sound of the rain falling and hitting the surrounding undergrowth and falling onto the roof of the tent. Give them a lead by making a sound yourself. When a steady sound is generated, tell the group to keep it going whilst you add the following ideas.

You listen to the rain but through it you can hear a faint sound that disturbs you. It is like nothing you have ever heard before, gradually it grows louder, coming closer and closer. As you walk round amongst the group quickly pick 4-5 of them to make the sound of the approaching noise whilst the others continue to make the rain. Build it up to a climax.

You can obviously vary the scenario to make the location and therefore the sound different, e.g. they can be in the arctic, the desert etc.

2   Have everyone standing on their own. Ask them to imagine that they are going to have to cross a deep canyon. The only means of doing this is via a broken and very rickety wooden bridge that sways in the wind. They have no choice but to attempt to make the crossing. At a signal from you everyone begins to cross his or her imaginary bridge. (NB you can help create a good atmosphere by using your cassette recorder to play a background sound of the wind blowing – the Discography on (p. 116) will refer you to some suitable recorded material.)

3   Quickly ask for several groups of 5-6 people each. Allocate an area of the room to each group. What they all have to do is to repeat the scenario in 2 (above), but this time the group members cross one at a time, the first being encouraged by the rest, until, finally, the last one is over.

In the course of 3 (above) the students have unwittingly begun an important aspect of the work: showing and sharing. It is important that they recognize that working in this way does not involve the conventional performer and audience separation, with its negative associations of individual display and passive consumption. What is learnt is learnt through *participation*, and the students learn from one another quite as much as from their teacher.

Speaking the text

After 10-15 minutes start the process of putting Puck's speech back together as a single unbroken unit of choric speech.

As before, get the class moving about experimenting with speaking their lines in as many different ways as possible. By now they will be familiar with this exercise and, as their confidence increases, the level of experimentation and risk taking should develop. When you are reasonably confident that everyone has at least a general idea of the words of his or her phrase, initiate an improvisation that will involve them speaking their lines and *only* their lines. This can be done in the following way:

1   Divide the group into sets of 6-8 people.

2   Ask them to imagine a situation of conflict. For instance, tell them to enact what might happen if they have been out visiting a friend's house and return home much later than they promised. It so happens that not only their parents await them, but also other brothers and sisters, plus (a surprise visit!) aunts, uncles, and cousins.

3   As the student chosen to play the 'culprit' enters the house, the others act out the parts of those waiting at home. Some are cross and demand an explanation or apology (Mum/Dad); others, when listening to the excuses, side with the late-comer against his or her parents. Eventually a full scale row breaks out amongst the family.

All this has to be done using *only* the text from Puck's speech. Thus tone, delivery and impact of the phrase or line all contribute to the meaning. It is helpful, though not necessary, if the erring child has the opening line, though he or she need not be the first to speak. Lines may be repeated as often as necessary.

When the improvisation seems finished, you can, if you wish, then ask the groups to show one another how they have used the text in this scenario. Then bring all the group together in a circle and place its members in the order in which their lines come in the speech itself. Thus the person on your right has the first line, the person on his or her right the second and so on. Simply explain that all you want at this stage is to establish that everybody knows the correct order of speaking and that they are going to say the lines round the circle in sequence. You will probably need to do this several times.

Once you are satisfied that they can more or less deliver the lines in order and that everyone knows more or less accurately what it is that they are supposed to say, it is time to introduce the percussion element. Incidentally, don't be pedantic as it doesn't matter at all if everyone is not word perfect as long as each can convey the essence of the line in his or her head.

Adding percussion

The percussion instruments are used to make a theatrical, aural context for speaking the lines from this part of the play. You will find it interesting to hear the kinds of sounds they produce and to remind them of their opening discussion about fairies. They will be impressed by the way in which the lines are transformed through the double action of speaking and accompanying the words.

The exercise again begins with a circle.

1 Give each student an instrument and explain that you want to explore making the kinds of sounds they associate with the other, fairy, world.

2 It will probably help the atmosphere if, during this work, you have the room darkened, and also select a suitably 'spooky' piece of music, perhaps from Vangelis' *Invisible Connections* (see Discography p. 116) with which to begin. As the group begin to make sounds with the instruments so you can decrease the volume of the tape.

3 If you are working with a large class (25+), you might decide to split them into two halves and have one half work on creating appropriate sounds whilst the others develop corresponding movements based on the previous exercises. If you do introduce movement, try to get the students to think of ways of moving which both correspond to the percussion sounds and which feel appropriate to the mood suggested by the words.

4 When they are ready and can combine sound and motion, distribute Puck's speech to one half of the group only. They should now be able to speak it chorically whilst the other half accompanies the speech with appropriate atmospheric sounds from their percussion instruments.

There is obviously a lot of scope for trial and error in all this. Be patient and don't expect too much too quickly. Once the group can successfully combine the words spoken by Puck with the sounds made by the percussion, you will probably want to try different things out such as getting the speakers to pause briefly between each line whilst the space is filled by the musicians. You could add a third layer: the recordings made in Session 2 could be played.

Follow-up work

When closing this session, get the students to talk about how Shakespeare's fairies seem to differ from some of the more conventional largely nineteenth century descriptions that they have looked at previously. To encourage and stimulate the discussion you might draw their attention to the representation of supernatural forces in popular culture, for example at the creation of E. T.. Let them also talk about what they think the fairies in *A Midsummer Night's Dream* should look like and their relationship to the 'real' or mortal world of the play. You could also ask a group to draw one or two of the fairy characters from the play and compare these efforts with those undertaken prior to beginning practical work.

Session 4

This session tackles a long speech of Titania's by breaking it down into manageable segments and then reassembling them through a series of games into a speech spoken by the whole group. Work on this speech *(II.1 81–117)* and the subsequent exercise both explore the darker side of the fairy world by concentrating on the language of conflict generated by the Oberon/Titania quarrel. Titania's speech, which talks of the disruption of the natural world brought about by her quarrel with Oberon, is more difficult than Puck's 'Now the hungry lion roars' which we encountered in the previous session. It is a classic example of the kind of language that young people find so difficult to negotiate; especially if it is being read aloud in class. Yet it is a speech full of strange and wonderful language, underpinned with a frightening malevolent power – just the sort of thing, in fact, to stir the blood of the sceptical adolescent. A group familiar with a practical approach, and who have undertaken choral speaking successfully, should be able to come to it with great effect. Moreover, it gives them some experience of dealing with an extended passage and seeing that they need not fear to move on in this way.

Preparation

1   Read Titania's speech beginning 'These are the forgeries of jealousy . . .' from *II. 1 81–117*. Also look out for any other parts of the play where the tensions within the fairy world are displayed.

2   Teach yourself or remind yourself of the refrain to *The Coventry Carol*.

3   Divide Titania's speech (I suggest how this could be done below) and distribute the lines or phrases in advance of the session. As

before, ask the pupils to try to learn their piece in advance. If the group is not large enough to manage the whole speech in one division take the first half and work on that, then add the second to it. It means the students have more to remember, but, in my experience, they do not find this particularly difficult as long as you approach the work one step at a time.

4 Bring a cassette recorder with a pre-recorded tape of some period music, preferably sounding formal and stately. (See Discography p. 116 for suggestions.)

Timing

The session can either be done as a double period (minimum 70 minutes) or divided into two sessions.

Starting practical work

Begin the session as usual with some of the warming up exercises and then begin to set up scenarios which help the learning of the lines and which encourage the pupils to find inventive ways of saying them. (See those used in the previous session for Puck's speech.)

Once they have grasped their line(s), what Titania says should prove a fruitful stimulus for further discussion and as the basis for written project work.

I have divided the speech as shown here but, as with almost everything else in this book, it is intended only as a suggestion. You may well discover alternative and more effective ways of distributing it amongst your class.

> These are the forgeries of jealousy://
> And never, since the middle summer's spring,
> Met we on hill,//in dale, forest, or mead,
> By paved fountain, or by rushy brook,//
> Or in the beached margent of the sea,//
> To dance our ringlets to the whistling wind,//
> But **with thy brawls thou hast disturb'd our sport.**//
> Therefore the winds, piping to us in vain,
> As in revenge,//have suck'd up from the sea
> Contagious fogs//which, falling in the land,
> Hath every pelting river made so proud//

That they have overborne their continents://
The ox hath therefore stretch'd his yoke in vain,//
The ploughman lost his sweat,//and the green corn
Hath rotted ere his youth attain'd a beard://
The fold stands empty in the drowned field,//
And crows are fatted with the murrion flock;//
The nine-men's-morris is fill'd up with mud,//
And the quaint mazes in the wanton green//
For lack of tread are undistinguishable.//
The human mortals want their winter cheer://
No night is now with hymn or carol blest.//
Therefore the moon, the governess of floods,
Pale in her anger,//washes all the air,
That rheumatic diseases do abound://
And thorough this distemperature we see
The seasons alter://hoary-headed frosts
Fall in the fresh lap of the crimson rose,//
And on old Hiems' thin and icy crown
An odorous chaplet of sweet summer buds//
Is, as in mockery, set.//The spring, the summer,
The childing autumn, angry winter, change
Their wonted liveries,//and the mazed world,
By their increase, now knows not which is which.//
And this same progeny of evils comes
From our debate,//from our dissension://
We are their parents and original.

(II.1 81-117)

The highlighted phrases could possibly be said in unison. Also do encourage the group to explore where they think pauses are needed, either in the speech as a whole or in an individual line. For example, in the penultimate line, adding a long pause before 'dissension' may have the effect of suggesting that Titania's language contains sorrow and regret as opposed to simple anger. Indeed, the quarrel itself could prove a useful focus for the attentions of the group.

The next exercise (which takes the form of a game) can be used whether or not you decide at this stage to attempt a speech as long as Titania's. You could also decide, if you wish, to start this session with it, using the longer more complicated text as a follow-on. Like the work on Titania's speech, the objective here is also to explore the quarrel of the fairy King and Queen. This is achieved by distributing to the group some of the adjectives thrown at one another by Oberon and Titania in this same scene.

1 Write the words listed below on scraps of paper and then ask everyone to draw out a word from a hat.

2 Tell them to keep the word to themselves for the time being.

3 Next set the mood by playing some stately Elizabethan music. (See Discography p. 116 for suggestions.)

4 Get the group to move around the room to this as if on display, imagining that they are wearing fine and expensive clothes. They are to greet one another with all the physical elegance they can manage but during the formal greeting (a bow or curtsey perhaps), they insult the person they are greeting by using their word.

Take the following words for the insults:

jealousy	proud
brawls	rash
revenge	contagious
drowned	mud
floods	anger
rheumatic	diseases
odorous	evils
rotted	empty

[The session can be broken at this point if you lack sufficient time to go further.]

Finally, I want to suggest an exercise on the play involving the whole group. It uses a simple song with movement and a little speaking of the text. This exercise, particularly if it is used in juxtaposition with that based on Titania's hostile speech to Oberon, shows the fairy world in an altogether different, more gentle and benign light. I want to look at the episode at the beginning of II.2, where Titania is sung to sleep by her attendant fairies. This is the text (the highlighted and numbered lines are those to be spoken by the group):

Titania:

Come, now a roundel and a fairy song,
Then, for the third part of a minute, hence:
Some to kill cankers in the musk-rose buds,
Some war with reremice for their leathern wings
To make my small elves coats, and some keep back

The clamorous owl, that nightly hoots, and wonders
At our quaint spirits. Sing me now asleep;
Then to your offices, and let me rest.

The Fairies sing.

You spotted snakes with double tongue,//
Thorny hedgehogs, be not seen;//
Newts and blind-worms, do no wrong,//
Come not near our fairy queen.//

Philomel, with melody,
Sing in our sweet lullaby;
Lulla, lulla, lullaby; lulla, lulla, lullaby.

Never harm,//
Nor spell,//
nor charm,//
Come our lovely lady nigh;//
So good night,//
with lullaby.
Weaving spiders come not here;//
Hence, you long-legg'd spinners, hence!//
Beetles black, approach not near;//
Worm nor snail, do no offence.//

Philomel, with melody,
Sing in our sweet lullaby;
Lulla, lulla, lullaby; lulla, lulla, lullaby.
Never harm,
Nor spell, nor charm,
Come our lovely lady nigh;
So good night with lullaby.

Fairy:

Hence, away! Now all is well.
One aloof stand sentinel.

If you have more students than you have lines, simply assign the same line(s) to more than one person. It doesn't matter as they will certainly be said differently.

1   First of all, you will need to teach all the group a basic fairy song. I suggest the words you use for it are taken from the fairy chorus. Instead of attempting to sing the whole of the verse twice, simply

take the one word 'Lulla' and use that as the basis for the song. If you pronounce it lu-lay, it fits easily into the well known *Coventry carol*. It is a very straightforward but pretty melody. If you are lucky some of the group will know it already.

2 Sitting in the by now accustomed circle, teach all the group the melody. Although the prospect may seem nerve racking, it is a very simple tune and easily recalled. You could, of course, ask a colleague in the music department to teach it to them in a previous lesson, but almost anyone who can hum a tune will cope. When they can all hum it satisfactorily, add the single word to be sung, 'lu-lay'.

3 Your next task is to distribute, either at random or in order so that it can be said chorically, the highlighted words (in bold) from the text on p. 47. Either way should be effective.

4 Then, using the class, construct an account of what is happening in this scene: the Queen and her courtiers have reached a clearing in the forest. Titania is tired and wants to rest; she asks the fairies to sing her to sleep. Select one person to represent Titania. It would be interesting, if you have the nerve, to represent her yourself. You could even decide to say Titania's speech, then you will be really sharing in the creation of the work and not simply controlling and directing it.

5 Tell the group that they must lead in their tired mistress and then, very gently, help her to lie down on the ground. Each one of them must then do one simple task in order to try to make her more comfortable. Groups familiar with this work usually respond by taking off their own jackets or cardigans and using them to cushion Titania. They will also often smooth her hair and generally 'tuck her in'.

6 As they are beginning to complete this task, get one of them to start singing the song, softly and slowly. Gradually the others should join in until they are all singing a gentle lullaby. They should then move out and form a circle around the sleeping Titania, all the while singing softly.

7 Then, at a signal (if you are representing Titania choose someone to begin speaking before you go into 'role'), that person speaks the first line. As she or he does so, they move in to the sleeping figure and make some gesture to the still figure. Leave it to the individual what that gesture might be, saying only that it is as if you wish to say farewell to someone you love and at the same time want to offer them a gift. One by one, the group should go to Titania, saying their

line in any way they feel appropriate. As they are doing this, they also make a physical gesture of farewell: a wave, a bow, a blown kiss, a light touch with the hand on Titania's forehead and so on. As each member of the group makes this gesture, the rest sustain the mood by softly singing the lullaby.

8   When everyone has finished, the person who began the speaking leads the group away, still singing. Let them go to the furthest point of the room and, if they can sustain it, sing more and more softly until the tune almost fades away.

I realize that some teachers will anticipate problems in trying to get a large group of fifteen-year-olds to sing, let alone sing softly. But remember that this is not the first practical session that you have had together; they are, or should be, prepared to some extent to cope. Singing the melody as a background to the action and speaking is not so very different from making the sound of the wind/rain which we essayed at the beginning of Session 3. But, if having to vocalise the word 'Lu-lay' appears to be jeopardizing an otherwise successful exercise, simply drop the word and have them all hum the melody.

Follow-up work

As in all the practical work, the way in which it is followed up in discussion will depend to a large extent on the ages of the students with whom you are working. But any age group could and should be asked which words and/or images stand out from the rest. You might also get them to talk about dreams and dreaming, and in doing so point out that this is a time in the action of the play where both fairies and mortals fall asleep.

In the section on *Romeo and Juliet*, we will adapt this last exercise to explore a very different situation.

Romeo and Juliet

Like *A Midsummer Night's Dream*, *Romeo and Juliet* is also often the play chosen by adults as being suitable for a young person's first direct encounter with Shakespeare. To be sure, the play is concerned with adolescence but it is frequently diminished by emphasizing romance rather than tragedy. The following exercises explore the tragic dimension of the text. Once again they are designed for use by the whole class working together and should be spread over at least two 70 minute sessions.

Session 1

The work is based on 1. 5, the Ball in Capulet's house. Potentially this is one of the most spectacular moments in the entire play. It involves music, dance, and the wearing of masks, and is the occasion on which Romeo and Juliet meet for the first time.

Preparation

1   You need a good quality cassette tape recorder, preferably portable. Get the very best sound equipment you can: you will need good volume, and clarity of sound helps enormously in getting the right atmosphere and mood.

2   You will need a pre-recorded tape containing dance music preferably from the Renaissance period, and two songs that reflect the general melancholy mood of the end of the play. (The Discography on p. 116 makes specific suggestions.) At some point you might want to ask the class to think of suitable music, and to bring in a record or a tape for you to play. However, when starting out on this exercise, it is probably better to provide the music yourself to give the appropriate mood and atmosphere for a formal dance. You can use 'pop' music very successfully, but not yet!

Renaissance music (such as that by the English composer William Byrd) is best at this stage. It was the popular dance music of its day, and Byrd was a contemporary of Shakespeare. You can easily find examples of his work, and also that of other Elizabethan/Jacobean composers recorded on reproductions of original instruments. (In the Discography on p. 116 you will find a list of contemporary recordings that I have found useful.) Whatever piece of music you choose for this exercise, it should have a strong rhythm.

3   Although the dance that forms part of the first exercise is not particularly difficult for a group to undertake, it will be a lot easier for them
if you know what you are doing! I suggest that, before trying it out
on a large group, you work through the instructions with a colleague
or with a small group of adults or cooperative students.

4   If no prior work has been done on the text, I suggest you consider
showing Zeffirelli's film of the play. It needs no introduction and,
although now over twenty years old, still packs a heavy emotional
punch. If this is impossible, tell the story in your own words up to
the point in Act I when the Ball begins.

5   You will need plain masks (one for each member of the group) that
can be tied securely to the head, and that have reasonably large holes
cut for both eyes and mouth. You will obviously have to alert the
students beforehand if you want them to provide masks themselves.
However you obtain them, it is important that the masks are plain
and undecorated. They can be either half or full face, but you should
decide which, as all the students should wear roughly identical
masks. The masks should tie on easily and securely. The reason for
wearing masks is that they can temporarily de-personalize individuals
and, as a result, generate less inhibited responses, particularly those
involving the expressive use of the body.

Timing

For almost all of these exercises you will need a minimum of one
unbroken hour.

Using dance

Shakespeare frequently used dance to conclude the comedies where it
represents harmony and reconciliation. Its use in this early tragedy seems
therefore interesting and full of theatrical potential.

The kind of dance required for this practical exercise is one demanding self-discipline and control from its participants. It should emulate the
purpose of the actual dance in the play: an excuse for a formal ritual of
display. But that ritual, like the society from which it springs, barely contains much stronger and potentially anarchic forces working within it, for
in this scene you have the polarized extremes of emotion expressed by
Romeo's love for Juliet, and by Tybalt's hatred of Romeo. These two

extremes can be juxtaposed within the context of a formal but elegant dance. The first task is therefore to teach the group a simple Renaissance dance.

As we noted in the section requiring singing in *A Midsummer Night's Dream,* you might anticipate problems here with recalcitrant 14-16 year olds. However, in my experience, this is not generally a problem, particularly if you stress that the moves are difficult to achieve, and lower the light level to avoid too much overt self-consciousness. If self-consciousness remains a distracting problem, have the group put on their masks whilst the dance is learnt. Remind the sceptical that this is the sixteenth century equivalent of modern disco dancing.

Starting practical work

1 Begin with everyone standing in a circle facing inwards. Make sure the numbers in the circle are even.

2 Nominate partners and decide which of the pair should represent the male and which the female.

3 Stress that this is a dance of display; the object being for each dancer to show off and attempt to out-shine the others in terms of his or her dancing and the extravagance of their imaginary costumes. During the dance both partners should seek to assert their social superiority by looks and bearing. You may wish to choreograph your own dance rather than attempt to follow the one I am going to outline below, but if you do, I suggest that at this stage you create a formal dance that will require a certain amount of concentration and cooperation to get right, rather than a freer, more spontaneous dance such as most young people are probably used to.

4 Choose which dancers are to represent men, and then ask them to follow this sequence:

   i Greet the whole circle of the dance by giving a formal bow.

   ii Imagine (or have, if eventually you decide to embellish the work by using costume) that you are wearing a large-brimmed hat.

   iii Raise the right hand and grasp the brim of the hat between thumb and fore-finger. Then, in an extravagant gesture, sweep the hat off the head and bring it down in an arc to a point over the left knee, accompanying the gesture with a deep bow.

iv Take the weight onto the left foot and then take a small hop back.

v Transfer the weight onto the right foot, pointing the left foot out in front whilst sweeping the hat across the body.

vi Keeping the weight on the right foot, place the hat elegantly back on the head and, bringing both feet together, come to an upright stance.

The task for the women is simpler. After the men have bowed, they respond by making a deep curtsy:

i Place the right foot immediately behind the left and, keeping the back straight, bend both knees and sink slowly down as far as possible without losing balance.

ii Slowly come back up to a standing position.

5 Both the movements of the male and the female should be done whilst facing in towards the middle of the circle. The men all move together (first), followed by all the women. When the introductions are complete, it is time to learn the basic dance steps.

6 All the dancers are now facing in towards the middle of the circle. When the formal greetings are completed, they all rise up onto the balls of their feet, and swivel in towards their partners. Once they are face to face, they sink gently down and distribute their weight evenly.

7 Both partners raise their right hands, palms facing outwards.

8 The dancers then lead off on the right foot and meet their partners by touching palm to palm.

9 They then move past their partners. As they do so, they raise their left hand (palm again outwards) and move on round the circle towards the oncoming dancer. They then meet left palm to left palm, pass each other as before, and so on, alternating right and left palm, until they meet their partner once again.

Once you have got this far satisfactorily, it is time to introduce some music.

Adding music

Start off by playing a few minutes of the music and by asking everyone to sit and listen to it and imagine the scene at Capulet's house. Then get them up on their feet with the same partner with whom they earlier rehearsed the dance. The 'man' should hold out his right arm in front of him, with the palm facing towards the floor; the 'woman' should then gently allow her hand to rest on the man's and together they should move around the room in time to the music.

Distribute the following lines, making sure as far as possible that each person does *not* know what the others are going to say. The distribution of the lines should be *random*, there is no set sequence. (If time is really a problem, then distribute the lines at the end of a previous session setting the task of having to remember them for this one. However, this does carry its own risk as you can never be sure that all those given lines will turn up to speak them.)

1 O, she doth teach the torches to burn bright!
2 Fetch me my rapier, boy.
3 It seems she hangs upon the cheek of night/
4 As a rich jewel in an Ethiop's ear:
5 To strike him dead I hold it not a sin.
6 Beauty too rich for use,
7 I'll not endure him.
8 I ne'er saw true beauty till this night.
9 this intrusion shall . . . convert to bitterest gall.
10 Did my heart love till now?
11 dares the slave/Come hither,
12 such a villain is a guest;   *(I.5 43-91)*

When each person has a line (it doesn't matter if two or more have the same line), re-form the circle ready to start the dance.

At this point, if you possibly can, it will help the sense of theatricality if you turn down the lights and tell the dancers to imagine that this ball takes place at night in a house lit by torches.

Tell them that they are to speak their line softly but clearly in the following sequence:

1 The 'male' partner raises his right hand to meet the oncoming left palm of his female partner and as they touch, he speaks and she listens.

2 Going on round the circle, he then leaves his partner behind and the on-coming dancer (female) now speaks to him and it is his turn to

listen. This alternation continues until the original partner is encountered once more.

3   Thus, the men speak first and the women listen; then the women speak and the men listen. In this way all the lines will be heard in the context of the formal dance of display.

4   When half way round the circle, the original partners meet again, either ending the dance with a bow or curtsey to one another or rotating in a half circle so that they face back the way in which they have come.

The dance can then be repeated again with the male leading off, but starting this time with his *left* palm raised to meet the right palm of his oncoming partner. As they return to their starting positions, they repeat their lines.

Tybalt remarks that Romeo and his friends have come to the Ball 'cover'd with an antic face' (55), in other words masked. You can take this up and incorporate it in the exercise.

Adding masks

Wearing their masks, and with their lines in their minds, get the group into a circle, dim the light, switch on the music, and begin the dance. The combination of all these elements is designed to give a sense of theatre and of excitement in speaking lines written by Shakespeare in a simple theatrical context that the group (and you) have made for themselves.

Follow-up work

When the dance is completed, sit down on the floor with everyone and ask what they heard. Which words or phrases can they recall? What did they think of the combination of music, dance and spoken language?

The group could now be divided into three and each group asked to read the play together aloud up to and including the Ball scene. You should not seek to intervene in any of the groups' work unless they directly ask for your assistance. Ideally you should be able to take yourself off to a corner of the rom and leave them with the sense that they are responsible for their own work.

However, if this is too difficult to accomplish without the presence of a teacher in each group or if you feel it would take too long, then play a pre-recorded tape of I.1 to I.5, whilst they follow it in their copies of the text.

In fact, by introducing the use of pre-recorded material at this stage and in this context, it may well prompt many of the group to listen in their own time. All the plays are now readily available from record libraries on pre-recorded tape or disc. They can be a useful aid in encouraging thinking about the plays and how they are interpreted in performance.

Encourage the students to look particularly at the attitudes of the young males who people Shakespeare's Verona; especially at Romeo. Is he different from the others; if so, in what way?

Session 2

Thus far we have seen how to use fragments from the text reconstructed in a theatrical way using movement, masks and music. Still using *Romeo and Juliet,* I want now to look at how the group as a whole can approach another long piece of text, similar in scale of difficulty to that spoken by Titania in II.1 of *A Midsummer Night's Dream,* which we explored in the first part of this chapter. The objective behind the exercise is to enable young people to talk about mood, meaning, metaphor, context and much more.

Preparation

In a more formal and literary classroom approach to reading Shakespeare one major problem encountered by teachers is how to encourage the students to make sense of long and often complex soliloquies. One of the best and also most difficult, is Juliet's in III.2 when she is alone and longing for the night and therefore for Romeo. This exercise uses the choric method to explore the speech. It must therefore be broken down into manageable fragments. As in previous exercises, these will eventually be reconstructed by the group.

1 Prepare and bring a pre-recorded tape containing two contemporary melancholy songs. (See the Discography p. 116.)

2 Re-read Juliet's soliloquy from III.2 1-31 'Gallop apace, you fiery-footed steeds . . .' and divide it for choric speaking.

When dividing this or any other soliloquy or passage from the plays as part of your preparation, the punctuation of the modern edition of the play you are using will be a help. However, don't feel enslaved by it; it is a guide to sense, but no more than that. Breaking a line up by a pause may get in the way of the verse, but it may also reveal a new meaning. In fact, once you have satisfactorily completed a choric reading of a soliloquy, an excellent follow-up exercise is to ask the group to do their own preparation for speaking chorically. One exercise I have used is to make a photocopy of the speech with the punctuation 'tippexed' out. Students are then asked to break it down into manageable units that nevertheless must continue to carry meaning(s).

I have divided up the speech to give each speaker slightly more to say than in previous exercises. Because it is a very complicated speech and some of the sections have to be longer than others, this is another case where it would be wise to distribute the lines to the group before the practical class. One way of breaking up the text for a group of 24+ would be:

> Gallop apace, you fiery-footed steeds,
> Towards Phoebus' lodging;// such a waggoner
> As Phaeton would whip you to the west,//
> And bring in cloudy night immediately.//
> Spread thy close curtain, love-performing night,//
> That runaway's eyes may wink,//and Romeo
> Leap to these arms//untalk'd of and unseen!//
> Lovers can see to do their amorous rites
> By their own beauties;//or, if love be blind,
> It best agrees with night.//Come, civil night,
> Thou sober-suited matron, all in black,//
> And learn me how to lose a winning match,//
> Play'd for a pair of stainless maidenhoods://
> Hood my unmann'd blood, bating in my cheeks,//
> With thy black mantle;//till strange love, grown bold,//
> Think true love acted simple modesty.//
> Come, night!//Come, Romeo!//Come, thou day in night;//
> For thou wilt lie upon the wings of night//
> Whiter than new snow, on a raven's back.//
> Come, gentle night;//come, loving, black-brow'd night,//
> Give me my Romeo.//
>
> *(III.2 1-21)*

If you wish, this is a good place in which to stop. If you have a large group then go on:

> And when I shall die//
> Take him and cut him out in little stars,//
> And he will make the face of heaven so fine//
> That all the world will be in love with night,//
> And pay no worship to the garish sun.//
> O, I have bought, the mansion of a love,//
> But not possess'd it;//and, though I am sold,
> Not yet enjoy'd.//
>
> *(III.2 21-28)*

Although there are two more concluding lines, I would end the soliloquy at this point.

Starting practical work

Begin your session like *all* practical sessions with some of the exercises/games from Chapter 1 (p. 12)

1 Check that everyone knows what they have to say and remind them if necessary. Then, when you are ready to begin work on the text, start by having all the class moving freely around the room, avoiding any contact with one another. You can continue to use masks if you want.

2 Announce that when you clap your hands each member of the group should speak his or her line(s) very quietly, so that no one else can hear it. Then have the phrases shouted out loudly, as if trying to tell someone in the next room. Get them to sing it. Try elongating all the vowel sounds. They will have had some experience of this approach in the work on the sonnet outlined previously in Chapter 1 (p. 24) and you will also have been through the process yourself if you tried out the workshops on *A Midsummer Night's Dream*. During all these exercises and variations of them that you invent for yourself, remind the students to play with the sound the language makes and to experience it as a physical sensation, rather than being concerned at this stage with what it may or may not mean. Often the meaning of a line will emerge even from such a mechanical approach that seems only to explore the sounds and speech rhythms of the spoken text.

3   Divide the whole group to make three or four sub-groups of roughly
    equal numbers and have each find a space for themselves. Tell them
    that, until you say anything to the contrary, the only words they may
    speak are those you have given them: Juliet's soliloquy. The groups
    then have to rehearse and perform an improvisation.

    They are all to imagine themselves in a launderette. Some are sitting
    or standing waiting for their load to come out of the machine, some
    are busy folding sheets that they have taken out of the drier, some are
    trying to find the right change to operate the machines and so on.
    Then, for some reason which you don't specify, an argument breaks
    out between two people which eventually involves the whole of the
    launderette. Some join in enthusiastically on one side or another;
    others attempt to calm things down and restore order. Don't give
    the groups any time to think about the situation once you have
    described it to them. Tell them to get on with it!

    An alternative scenario would be: Tell the students to break into
    groups of 6–8 in number. They are to imagine themselves on a bus.
    A conductor is taking the fares when a foreign tourist asks for
    directions. The conductor responds but someone on the bus
    disagrees. This promotes an argument between the conductor and all
    the passengers, some of whom side with him, while others think him
    wrong. Whatever you use or create for yourself, try to ensure that it
    requires maximum participation from all the group in roughly equal
    measure.

4   After a few minutes, during which time chaos of a kind will develop,
    choose a group which has been working reasonably well on the
    scenario and ask the others to stop and watch them perform. Then,
    watch the second group and so on until all the groups have displayed
    their work and publicly spoken Shakespeare's language. Allow all the
    participants to look and listen to what is happening and thus begin to
    become used to being watched as they play and speak words written
    by Shakespeare.

5   Move back into a circle, all looking towards the centre, and try put-
    ting all the lines back together in sequence. It will help if you have
    the students stand in order of speaking with the first line, as it were,
    on your immediate right and the last line on your immediate left.
    Then, with you acting as prompter, get them to speak in sequence,
    trying gradually to speed up the pace. This will take some time and
    patience on behalf of everyone but shouldn't prove too difficult,
    even if you are attempting the whole of the soliloquy.

6   When you and they are happy that the sequence has been memorized and that each participant has learned his or her line more-or-less accurately, break the circle up and get them moving about the room. Begin with a slow pace then move into a brisk walk, avoiding any physical contact. At a signal from you, try out the speaking of the sequence whilst the group moves about the room. Tell them the only thing they have to think about is the right moment for their line and to be sure that all the group gets to hear it! With you in the role of prompter (you will probably know the whole of the soliloquy your-self by now), gradually increase the speed at which the students are moving. The first time through is at a brisk walking pace, the second at a trotting or jogging pace, and the third as fast as they can safely move about the room whilst avoiding running into one another. Really push them physically and you will find that the urgency of the movement is fed through into the spoken text.

7   Carry the exercise on until they are all exhausted from running and speaking; then, urging them all the time to concentrate on what they are doing, quickly bring them together into a very close group facing outwards with eyes shut. Tell them that they are to repeat their lines from the soliloquy but this time they have to whisper it just loudly enough so that all the group can hear. Repeat this and then form the group into a circle, facing inwards. All holding hands, they should sink down onto their knees, drop hands and say the soliloquy as if telling a story to the others in the group. Stress that it is a vitally important story and that each individual must say his or her line in a way that really makes the others listen. Encourage them to use ges-tures and eye contact. Repeat this at least two or three times, getting them to imagine that Juliet's father is just outside the door and she can barely restrain herself from yelling out in excitement and anticipation.

Further exercises

At the end of these exercises designed to explore the soliloquy, you will find the group will be both excited and stimulated enough to want to discuss not only what individual lines mean but also what the mood of the speech is and what is happening to Juliet at this point in the play. The repetition of the word 'night', the prefiguration of her own death ('And when I shall die'), and perhaps above all the extraordinary energy that drives the speech along until at 'Give me my Romeo,' it stops, draws breath and becomes reflective, should now become an eager subject for discussion and analysis.

You can use the practical approaches outlined in this chapter to focus on other speeches in the play, perhaps working towards running them together to scan the development of Juliet's emotional life. For example, Juliet's speech in IV.3 15-59, in which she contemplates taking the Friar's potion, offers some terrific material that you could use. You could make use of the percussion instruments whose use was discussed in the *A Midsummer Night's Dream* section (p. 41) to make a suitably eerie backdrop to lines like these:

1 I have a faint cold fear thrills through my veins,
  That almost freezes up the heat of life.
2 What if this mixture do not work at all?
3 What if it be a poison, . . .
4 How if, when I am laid into the tomb,
  I wake before the time that Romeo
  Come to redeem me? . . .
5 Shall I not then be stifled in the vault,
6 To whose foul mouth no healthsome air breathes in,
7 And there die strangl'd ere my Romeo comes?
8 . . . bloody Tybalt, yet but green in earth,
9 Lies festering in his shroud; . . .
10 At some hours in the night spirits resort!
11 . . . loathsome smells, . . .
12 . . . shrieks like mandrakes torn out of the earth,
13 . . . living mortals, hearing them, run mad:
14 . . . shall I not . . . pluck the mangled Tybalt from
  his shroud?
15 . . . with a club, dash out my desperate brains?

You can also ask the students themselves, again working in groups, to select some shorter speeches on which to work before presenting the results to the rest of the class. It would be interesting to have one group working on Romeo's thoughts on love before he has met Juliet; for example:

Love is a smoke made with the fume of sighs;
Being purg'd, a fire sparkling in lovers' eyes;
Being vex'd, a sea nourish'd with lovers' tears.
What is it else? A madness most discreet,
A choking gall, and a preserving sweet.
                              (I.1 188-192)

Other groups can go through the text carefully and draw together lines that attempt to deflate such romantic excess: see in particular the text of Benvolio and Mercutio in I.1, 2, 4 and 5.

In the work in Part 1 on *A Midsummer Night's Dream,* we used practical exercises to explore two very different episodes in the life of the fairy kingdom. Thus far in *Romeo and Juliet* we have looked at the excitement and anticipation that accompanies adolescent love and at the tensions and extremes of emotion that are barely held in check at the beginning of the play and which explode towards the end with tragic consequences.

To conclude Session 2, therefore, I want to look at the deaths of children that are at the heart of the play. The previous work on Juliet's soliloquy involved a good deal of physical exertion. In teaching through practical work it is usually a good idea to follow any energetic expressive exercise by something that is calmer and more reflective.

1   Get the students to lie down on their backs on the floor in a circle with their heads facing towards the centre. Go through a simple relaxation exercise with them:

   i   Stretch your body as far as you can . . . hold it . . . relax.

   ii   Repeat the stretching.

   iii   Eyes closed. Think of your body as being very heavy . . . you can't lift it off the ground even if you wanted to. Try to relax every bit of it as follows: toes, feet, ankles, knees, legs, thighs, back, shoulders, fingers, hands, arms, kneck, head, eyes.

This should take 3-4 minutes.

2   When they are all lying quietly, tell them that you want them to listen to a song. Explain that the song explores the emotions associated with the loss of a loved one. I use *Fortune my Foe,* an anonymous Elizabethan ballad which was enormously popular at the time and subsequently. (See the Discography p. 116 for where to find a recording of it.)

> Fortune my foe,
> Why dost thou trouble me?
> And with thy favours
> Never greater be.
> Wilt thou, I say,
> Forever breed me pain?

If you use your own recording of another song, it is important that the mood of the piece and, if possible the lyrics too, match the mood of emotion generated in IV.5 when the parents of Juliet, her nurse and the Count Paris discover the drugged body of the young woman and believe her to be dead.

3 Before you actually start the music, remind the students what happens in IV.5 and tell them to think about the tragic outcome of this play as they listen.

4 The song lasts for about four minutes. Whilst it is playing, darken the room and light a candle and place it in the centre of the room.

5 When the song is over, ask one person (preferably someone you know to be reasonably reliable and self-confident) to remain lying flat on the floor with eyes closed and hands folded across the chest. Move the candle to just in front of his or her head.

6 Have the others get up slowly and form a ring around the 'body'. Tell them that the figure on the floor represents the body of Juliet (asleep, but presumed dead by those about to discover her).

7 Whilst they are doing this, quickly distribute the following lines taken from IV.5. The order in which they are subsequently spoken is unimportant.

> My child, my only life,
> She's dead,
> Alack the day!
> She's cold;
> O woeful time!
> Life, living, all is Death's!
> hateful day!
> one poor and loving child,
> But one thing to rejoice and solace in,
> woeful day!
> Never was seen so black a day as this:
> slain!
> O love!
> kill'd!
> O child!
> My soul,
> Dead art thou!
> Alack, my child is dead,
> with my child my joys are buried!

8   Explain that upon a signal from you (a light touch on the shoulder) the group should approach the body one by one, kneel beside it, say the short piece of text aloud, and make a gesture of farewell to the 'dead' girl. When one person is returning to the circle, signal the next to move forward. Explain that the gesture is as important as the words, and can take whatever form seems appropriate: a light touch on the forehead or the hands, or, perhaps it may involve the giving of a real or imagined gift: a ring, bracelet, necklace.

9   As this exercise is progressing play a second melancholic song. I use one entitled *Three Ravens* which, like the first, reflects the Elizabethan taste for melancholia and at the same time, mirrors in song the mood and events that the stage action of this scene narrates. If you are working with a large group this exercise can take some time, and it is wise to have some additional music pre-recorded to follow *Three Ravens*. It does not have to be period music, I have recently used Jessye Norman singing one of Richard Strauss' *Four Last Songs*.

10   When everyone or as many people as you decide to call, have, as it were, bid farewell to Juliet, fade the music down to silence. Then, after a brief pause and in the silence it creates, have seven voices speak the following epilogue (distributed to seven people selected before the exercise):

> All things that we ordained festival,//
> Turn from their office to black funeral;//
> Our instruments to melancholy bells,//
> Our wedding cheer to a sad burial feast,//
> Our solemn hymns to sullen dirges change,//
> Our bridal flowers serve for a buried corse,//
> And all things change them to the contrary.
> *(IV.5 84-90)*

Alternatively, as you have been controlling the whole process as an outsider, you might want to speak the concluding lines yourself. After they have been spoken, leave another brief pause to let them sink in before setting in motion the changes needed to prepare for a follow-up discussion.

All the students should be involved in changing the scene and the atmosphere by pulling back any closed curtains and coming together to sit in a circle with you on the floor. It is always important to leave time to discuss the results of practical work for it often carries an emotional charge that the students need to negotiate with you and with one another. It may well be that exercises such as this last one are too emotionally difficult for some students, and they will express this by withdrawing either physically or emotionally. In this case such people may attempt to disrupt the others by laughter or giggling. Both responses are a perfectly legitimate, if tiresome, defence mechanism. But if individuals threaten to disrupt the majority, just ask them to sit out and watch until the exercise ends.

Follow-up work

If the exercises on this play have begun to work, your students will have had some theatrical experiences which can greatly enhance understanding and enjoyment of the play. Their emotions have been engaged and they now have the necessary stimulus to engage their intellects in seeking to explore and develop the powerful direct experience of manufacturing meanings for themselves that your practical approach has given them. I suggest you begin the discussion by asking the person who represented Juliet what the exercise felt like to her or him.

In my experience it is rare to find a group who, after such a session, remain unresponsive. You need to direct and focus the energy of that response back onto issues contained within the text itself. Obvious areas for further discussion would be the attitude of the parents towards Juliet both before and after this scene, and also perhaps the way in which the young people in the play look at the world of Verona, and how their views and attitudes differ from those of their elders. Connections will inevitably be made between the personal experiences of the students and those of the characters in the play; the spoken language too can come in for more close scrutiny. You might, for example, read a short extract from *Hamlet* in which Laertes discovers that his sister is mad (IV.5 152-158) in order to illustrate that sometimes the more extreme the emotion, the simpler the language used by Shakespeare to express it.

Postscript

It is impossible to anticipate exactly how a practical session will work out and individuals will respond in very different ways. Don't despair if you don't immediately succeed in getting exactly the results you expect; certainly don't panic if from time to time you feel that you are losing control of the group. Working practically is probably a new experience for the class as it may be for you and both need time to come to terms with new demands and expectations.

The principal focus in both parts of this chapter has been on breaking down Shakespeare's language into manageable sections that can be committed to memory and then re-built into a whole through a series of games and exercises. But in addition to choric speech, there are other ingredients in this recipe that can be used in cooking up a practical approach to teaching Shakespeare. In subsequent chapters I will be looking at other methods and other texts, showing how both may be tackled with confidence by a teacher of English.

3

Practical Approaches to *Hamlet,* *Macbeth* and *Julius Caesar*

Hamlet

In the previous chapter, I demonstrated in some detail the basis of a particular practical approach to Shakespeare: using choric speech. I want now to illustrate some further practical strategies based on three different texts currently included on exam syllabuses. The first sessions are on *Hamlet,* one of the most frequently set Advanced Level texts.

A major concern of teachers, particularly those preparing their pupils for public examinations, is the exploration of character in Shakespeare. This is hardly surprising, given the number of questions in 'A' level papers that ask for character analysis. The sessions on *Hamlet* are therefore planned to create a focus on a particular character: Ophelia.

In studying the text in the classroom, the question of Hamlet's madness is often discussed: is he mad, or merely pretending to be? But in the case of Ophelia there is no doubt at all. She is not mad at the beginning of the play, but is driven into that state and eventually into taking her own life by what happens to her and to those whom she loves. The objective of the following practical exercises is to provoke a discussion of why and how she collapses into madness. To do this, I have selected from the main body of the text a series of individual words and phrases that are directed at Ophelia by the three most important men in her life: her father (Polonius), her brother (Laertes), and her lover (Hamlet). They are then brought together to provide the spoken text in the following exercise.

Timing

The first session could be done in a single period (35-45 minutes). The second could either be undertaken as a double session or split into two halves of roughly equal length.

Session 1

Preparation

1 Prepare lines from the text as outlined below and distribute them before the session.

2 Re-read all the episodes in the play which involve Ophelia.

3 Have a blindfold ready to be used.

4 Have a cassette player and a recording of some seventeenth century lute music. (See the Discography p. 116.)

5 If you are preparing an 'A' Level set then, in an earlier meeting, ask them to:

   a   Remind themselves of the gender of those responsible for the original representation of Ophelia on the Elizabethan stage. Ask them to think what implications this might have both then and if they were to see a boy playing Ophelia today.

   b   Read all the episodes in the play that involve Ophelia and Laertes, Polonius and Hamlet.

   c   Look at I.1 of *A Midsummer Night's Dream,* paying particular attention to the arguments of Egeus regarding what he sees as his daughter's duty (see especially lines 22-45) and also those of Theseus regarding the laws of Athens (65-78; 117-121).

Starting practical work

Bring the class together and, after you have gone through what you judge to be adequate introductory exercises in preparation for a practical session (see Chapter 1 p. 20), tell them that the objective of the session is to explore what happens to Ophelia. Together with some of the usual games and physical and vocal exercises, I suggest you include a brief improvisation on the following lines:

1 Have the group spaced out in the room sitting on the floor. Ask them to shut their eyes and recall what it was like in their school playground when they were aged 8-10. Ask them to recall games played, friends, teachers etc.

2   Now ask everyone to improvise being a young child in a playground.
    They can speak, run about, join with others or stay by themselves.

3   Let the improvisation run for two or three minutes and watch it
    carefully. See if any patterns emerge: who plays with who, who is
    alone, what kind of games?

4   Ask everyone to sit down again and ask one or two people what they
    remember of the playground. See if anyone mentions bullying
    and/or difficulties with authority figures such as teachers. Ask
    everyone about bullying. What do they remember about it from their
    earlier days at school? Were they bullied? Did they bully others? Ask
    one or two people to say of what the bullying consisted. Was it actual
    physical violence or the threat of violence? Was it verbal assault?
    (*What you are attempting to draw out here is that bullying does not
    have to be physical, that words can cause as much, if not greater harm
    and sense of personal humiliation.*)

Exploring the role of Ophelia

1   Choose someone to represent Ophelia. If you have a mixed group,
    choosing a boy to represent the role would be interesting; not only
    was the role originally played by a young man but it was of course
    written by a man and performed to an audience predominantly,
    although not exclusively, composed of men. This information is
    important when you come to the 'follow-up' discussion and issues
    such as the way in which women are represented in the play are
    discussed.

2   Allocate the following lines, one or two (depending on numbers) to
    each member of the group, excluding the person representing
    Ophelia. The text is taken from I.3 5-33 (Laertes); I.3 105-107,
    127, I.2 141-144, (Polonius); III.1 135-147, (Hamlet).

    1   the trifling of his favour,
    2   Hold it a fashion
    3   a toy in blood,
    4   Perhaps he loves you now,
    5   you must fear,
    6   weigh what loss your honour may sustain,
    7   Fear it, Ophelia,
    8   fear it, my dear sister;

9 think yourself a baby,
10 Do not believe his vows,
11 Lord Hamlet is a prince, out of thy star;
12 This must not be:
13 Admit no messengers,
14 receive no tokens.
15 be thou as chaste as ice,
16 Get thee to a nunnery:
17 marry a fool;
18 God hath given you one face, and you make yourselves another:
19 You gig,
20 you lisp,
21 [you] nickname God's creatures,
22 [you] make your wantonness your ignorance,
23 you speak like a green girl,

3   When you have done this, blindfold the student representing Ophelia. Lead him or her gently to the centre of the room away from the others and whisper what is going to happen. What happens next should not come as a surprise to 'Ophelia' as it otherwise can prove too disconcerting to the individual concerned. On returning to the main group, tell them that the object of the exercise is to make 'Ophelia' feel really uncomfortable, in fact to try to humiliate her. This is to be done *solely* by using the words they have been allocated and no others. They are to approach her as a group.

They may need some initial prompting from you but what usually happens is that most of them enthusiastically join in bullying 'Ophelia'. You will have to watch the progress of the exercise very carefully so that it doesn't get out of hand. Some students may find the exercise distasteful and remain on the periphery, refusing to take a full part. Make a mental note of who they are (and who takes to the role with enthusiasm) in order to bring this into the subsequent discussion.

4   After a few minutes, stop the exercise and take off the blindfold. Ask if anyone else would like to volunteer to take Ophelia's place. Carry the game on until you feel it has begun to grow stale (you don't have always to use a blindfold).

5   Sit all the participants down in a circle and ask them what they felt about the exercise. Start with those who were blindfolded.

What emerges is the extent to which they are now aware of the aggression behind so much of what is said to this young and vulnerable woman. It can, and indeed it should, lead on to further discussion of Ophelia's relationships with the three principal male figures in her life and may also raise broader issues surrounding the representation of women, not only in Shakespeare but also in contemporary society. Some students may also object that the words spoken to Ophelia have been taken out of context, and therefore distorted. If that happens all to the good. Make it a starting point for a future discussion in which the words just spoken are explored in the dramatic context supplied by Shakespeare.

After the discussion and to conclude the session, go further into the play (to IV.5) and examine what is said to Ophelia by her brother when, after arriving back in Elsinore, he learns of his father's death and sees for himself that his sister is mad. Allocate lines 156-162. There is no need to do this before the session and it doesn't matter if some of them are repeated or some of the group have merely to listen.

1   O rose of May
2   Dear Maid
3   kind sister
4   sweet Ophelia
5   O heavens
6   is't possible a young maid's wits
7   Should be as mortal as an old man's life
8   Do you see this?
9   O God!

1   Make a circle so that, with arms outstretched, all may comfortably hold hands. Find one or perhaps two new volunteers to represent the mad Ophelia. Ask them to stand in the middle of the circle and to do nothing except, without using any physical force, try to escape.

2   Ask all the participants to remember the scene (you can recall it for them) and to imagine that they are the hapless brother watching his mad sister, helpless with grief. Tell the group forming the circle that their task is simply to confine 'Ophelia' within the circle by joining hands to prevent her leaving.

3   As she moves around towards different individuals, their physical attempt to restrain her should be accompanied by whatever line(s)

they have to speak. The line itself can be directed at Ophelia, at someone else in the circle or said to themselves. You can if you wish change the 'Ophelia' and continue the exercise for a few more minutes.

4   During this exercise play the lute music softly in the background.

Follow-up work

Spend a few minutes at the end of the session exploring the contrast between the Laertes/Ophelia encounter at the beginning of I.3, and this from IV.5. Having focused on the lines from the text put together in a new sequence, your students probably see more clearly than before details of the play that frequently get submerged in a broad over-view of the text. Some of the things that have been said to Ophelia are quite horrific, but Laertes' line 'O rose of May, Dear maid, kind sister' has a wonderful directness and sincerity that, in my experience, often move the speakers and the listeners taking part in this exercise to real compassion. In discussion, it also raises the issue of who is really responsible for what happens to Ophelia.

Session 2

Preparation

1   Obtain a reproduction of John Everett Millais' painting *Ophelia* (Tate Gallery, London) depicting the scene described by Gertrude in IV.7.

2   If possible, have ready to screen the sections dealing with this same episode in one, or preferably both, versions of the play made by Laurence Olivier in 1948, and more recently, by Derek Jacobi and Rodney Bennett, for the BBC/Time Life series.

Starting practical work
Begin the session with the usual preparatory exercises, using voice and movement.

1   Distribute the text of Gertrude's speech to the group:

> There is a willow grows askant the brook//
> That shows his hoar leaves in the glassy stream//
> There with fantastic garlands did she come
> Of crow-flowers//nettles, daisies, and long purples//
> That liberal shepherds give a grosser name//
> But our cold maids do dead-men's-fingers call them//
> There on the pendent boughs//her crownet weeds
> Clambering to hang//an envious sliver broke//
> When down her weedy trophies and herself
> Fell in the weeping brook//Her clothes spread wide//
> And mermaid-like awhile they bore her up//
> Which time she chanted snatches of old lauds//
> As one incapable of her own distress//
> Or like a creature native and indu'd
> Unto that element//But long it could not be//
> Till that her garments, heavy with their drink//
> Pull'd the poor wretch from her melodius lay//
> To muddy death.
>
> *(IV.7 166-183)*

2   Rebuild the speech gradually, using the methods described in Chapter 2 (p. 43). When you feel that the group can speak it chorically have them do so several times.

3   Lower the lights as much as you can. Ask them to form a close circle on the floor, lying on their stomachs facing inwards.

4   Tell them first to imagine that they were the only witness of what happened to Ophelia, and are now informing others, although what they are relating must remain a terrible secret. It is a disgrace that must not be heard outside the immediate circle.

5   Then ask them to tell the story again, this time in the guise of a friend of Ophelia's, whose reaction is one of anger and frustration, coupled with grief. Like the previous version, this too must be done so that only those within the circle are privy to it.

6   Ask them now to tell the story as if mocking the action and fate of Ophelia.

7   Finally ask them to stop, to close their eyes and think of Gertrude. How would she have said this speech? When they are ready, have

them speak it in a whisper, imagining themselves in Gertrude's position.

[You could break the session here, after a discussion of the speech and the events which led to what it so graphically describes. However, if time permits, go straight on without discussing the speech to considering the representation of it in either (or both) of the two contrasting filmed versions of the play.]

8   If you can show both extracts, begin with the Olivier footage and follow it immediately with that taken from the BBC/Time Life production.

9   When both screenings are complete, pass around the reproduction of Millais' painting. Ask for comments on the representation of the action described in the text.

Given that the group have experienced in the previous session some of the things said to Ophelia by Hamlet, Laertes and Polonius, it will be interesting to see what they make of a variety of ways in which her death is represented. They have spoken the text written for Gertrude and listened to by Claudius and Laertes (one of the few occasions in the play when a female character is the sole focus of attention). They will also have looked and listened to the representation of Ophelia's suicide by at least two men (a painter and an actor/director) responsible for creating it on canvas and celluloid. Millais and Olivier both romanticize and sanitize the event. They create an image using only part of what Gertrude says. We are shown a young and still beautiful girl in no way disfigured by her madness. She lies relaxed, her long hair streaming out behind her, framing her face. She is bedecked with flowers, her clothes arranged decorously. There is nothing in either image of the muddy death when she is dragged to the bottom by the weight of her waterlogged clothes.

In the subsequent discussion, ensure that, if you have used the Olivier film, you re-run the section in which he films Ophelia floating down stream and have your finger on the pause button in order to stop it and see how the image relates to the 'voice-over': Gertrude's description of the event.

Follow-up work

You can follow-up a successful practical session with a more conventional approach.

The work done on Ophelia could usefully be extended by asking the group to sub-divide into three. One group's task would be to explore the relationship between Ophelia and her father; another group would explore that with her brother and the last would look at Ophelia and Hamlet. They should all be told to look carefully at the occasions in the play when Ophelia talks (or listens) to one or other of the three male characters. They should take notes and subsequently write about what appears to be happening and, more importantly, what significance they attach to it.

The groups should also be reminded to encompass all the occasions on which Ophelia is present, including that when it is only her lifeless corpse being represented. (I am thinking of the behaviour of Hamlet and Laertes at Ophelia's funeral (V.1).) They could also profitably consider how, if directing the play, they would show the character of Ophelia at any point in the action *not* indicated in the stage-directions of the modern text. If a group decides she could be shown, they will need to argue for what she would be doing; who, if anyone, she would be with, and explain the intention behind this addition to the text. For example, the stage directions of the first court scene (I.2) claim the presence of both her brother and her father; why is she absent? What interpretative opportunities are opened up if she is shown as being present?

Whilst one group presents their findings, the others should be encouraged to listen to the presentation of the argument before judging whether or not the conclusions are theatrically legitimate and consistent with their reading of the printed text. You can encourage the students to present their cases with the aid of notes but, to encourage spontaneity, they should not read aloud from a prepared essay. There is a lot to be gained from continuing to work in groups even when the emphasis of the work is more conventional. It encourages a sharing of ideas and a sense of collective commitment which spills over from the practical exercises themselves. Students can and should subsequently write up all their research findings.

Macbeth

The exercises I have outlined for this play are designed to explore the relationship between Lady Macbeth and Macbeth, the shifting balance of power between the two and the presentation of supernatural forces. Each exercise is designed to facilitate later group discussions and essays or course work relating to these aspects of the play. As in all the exercises I have suggested, it is not necessary always to follow the order in which I have written them. Only you can judge what would be of the greatest use to your students at any given moment and in relation to any on-going classroom work.

One of the most frequently set questions on this play asks candidates to consider how, if they were staging it, they would present the witches. Indeed, it is a problem that bedevils any director of this play and one that must be negotiated by teachers and students alike. How, in the second half of the twentieth century, should the physical embodiment of evil forces be made to look? How are they to be understood? Most students of this play will experience no difficulty in believing in the existence of evil (although they may not immediately call it that) and will point to famine and disease as examples of the way in which it is working in the world. They are also familiar with a popular language of representation in horror films, videos, and even cartoons such as *Transformers, Gem* etc.

The opening scene provides us with a good many opportunities for using improvisation as well as speaking the text. I suggest trying the exercises as a good way into the play as a whole. This will also lead into the more specific problem of how to represent the forces of evil: Shakespeare's three 'black and midnight hags', and determine their function in the text.

Timing

Each session could be taught in 35–45 minutes although both potentially contain sufficient material for twice that amount of time.

Session 1

Preparation

1 Make a tape-recording of a storm lasting 5-10 minutes; include thunder. (See Discography p. 116.)

2 Ask the students to bring simple face-masks that are *not* decorated and that can be tied securely round the head.

3 Bring a portable cassette recorder and a recording of music, perhaps by Vangelis or Jarre. (See Discography p. 116.)

Starting practical work

Start the work with the by now familiar introductory games, plus physical, and vocal warm up routines. Adapt the movement exercise described in 'Creatures' on p. 22: instead of asking them to make creatures they have never seen, ask them to move around the room on their own as creatures they know about, but don't like. For example, 'creepy crawlies' like spiders, wasps, mosquitoes, daddy-longlegs, bats, beetles, scorpions, toads, snakes etc. When they have done this add these activities:

1 Begin by having everyone standing, and then ask them each to take a partner. One person is to be 'blind', the other sighted. The 'blind' partner must keep his or her eyes tightly shut whilst their partner guides them around the space. Stress that the exercise must be conducted in silence, and that the guides can only use the most minimal physical contact to steer their charges around, e.g. the lightest of finger-tip touches to signal a change in direction, an order to stop, etc. The 'blind' partner must move *slowly.*

2 After a while change around so that the previously 'blind' partner now acts as guide. (You will have to keep your own eyes open to stop anyone getting hurt by bumping into people or objects!)

3 Have everyone seated. Ask for responses to the blind exercise. Lead on to introducing the fear of the dark. How many of them were afraid of the dark as young children? Why?

4 Staying seated ask about ghosts. Has anyone seen one? Do they believe in ghosts?

Now the imagination of the group has been stimulated, and they are working cooperatively, it is time to introduce some lines from the first scene of *Macbeth*.

5   Divide the group into small sections. (I am imagining a class of 30 and have therefore made five groups of six.) Distribute words or phrases to the groups, one word or phrase per person.

Group A: I come, Graymalkin!//When shall we three meet again? //Where the place!//Fair is foul//filthy air//In thunder//

Group B: When the hurlyburly's done//There to meet with Macbeth.//Hover through the fog//lightning//Paddock calls.// Anon.//

Group C: In rain//When the battle's lost and won.//Graymalkin //Upon the heath//foul is fair//filthy air//

Group D: set of sun//meet with Macbeth//lost and won//hover through the fog//hurlyburly//meet with Macbeth//

Group E: Graymalkin // Paddock //foul // lost// done // Macbeth//

6   Encourage the groups to move around the space experimentally using as background sound something abstract and other-worldly, perhaps from either Jean Michel Jarre or Vangelis or other composers whose music you think might prove effective in the context. Tell them to think of themselves as weird super-human creatures, perhaps from another planet and get them to use the sounds the words make as the expression of the creatures' different states: anger, happiness, calm, troubled, frightened etc.

7   Start off by having everyone moving on their own and keeping to their own space. Gradually you can bring people together into the five groups. Once all five groups are established and moving together (there should be a minimal physical contact between all six in a group), have them encounter other groups as they move about the space. Suggest that one meeting is between friends, another between enemies, another of mutually frightened creatures.

8   Above all, encourage the students to experiment with the sound of the language. Have them elongate the vowel sounds, hiss the word or phrase, say them fluidly, in bursts, singing, weeping, and so on. Sometimes just one person in a group will speak; at others all of them will speak their word or phrase together.

9   Now give each group the following:

1   When shall we three meet again
2   When the hurlyburly's done,

3 When the battle's lost and won,
4 That will be ere set of sun,
5 Where the place?

10 Tell each group to find a space together away from the other groups. Each group should rehearse saying the verse chorically. To do so they should sit in a circle on the floor facing inwards.

11 After a few minutes, during which you should visit each group to encourage them and check their progress, get all of them, in turn and without moving from their spot on the floor, to demonstrate to the rest how they speak the witches' text. When this is complete, bring everyone into one large circle.

12 Ask the class about the words they have been speaking, what sounds predominate (for example, the long 's' creates a hissing sound). If you have time, you could use subsequent verses. When lines are broken up in this way, the rhythm demands that certain words stand out (and in this instance appear to carry a sinister weight); for example, 'Hover', 'filthy', and 'lost'.

This kind of basic, virtually inevitable recognition is nonetheless valuable for an introduction to the play. You can use it to develop the sense of the supernatural, adding for good measure a pre-recorded tape of a storm with thunder and lightning. Also turn the light level down as far as you can without causing chaos. Try the exercise with and without the participants wearing masks.

13 After this work on abstract shapes and sounds linked to the text, try an improvisation which forces the group to approach the problem from a different perspective. Suggest that they think of a setting for the opening scene of *Macbeth* that suggests the boardroom inside a twentieth century office building belonging to a major company.

14 Re-form the earlier groups and divide the words of the scene between them. Again, they needn't be word perfect, but this time they should speak the words in the order in which they come.

15 Suggest they try to forget all about the previous work and instead imagine that they are very smartly dressed and full of self-confidence. The words should be spoken as if by a meeting of Mafia bosses. They are quiet, calm but deadly. Try to let the words themselves do the expressive work and see what happens.

The final exercise in this session is also connected to the supernatural and to witchcraft. It also prepares the students for the next session's focus on

Macbeth and Lady Macbeth. It consists in an exploration of the following speech of Lady Macbeth:

> . . . Come, you spirits
> That tend on mortal thoughts! unsex me here,
> And fill me from the crown to the toe top-full
> Of direst cruelty; make thick my blood,
> Stop up the access and passage to remorse,
> That no compunctious visitings of nature
> Shake my fell purpose, nor keep peace between
> Th'effect and it! Come to my woman's breasts,
> And take my milk for gall, you murdering ministers,
> Wherever in your sightless substances
> You wait on nature's mischief! Come, thick night,
> And pall thee in the dunnest smoke of hell,
> That my keen knife see not the wound it makes,
> Nor heaven peep through the blanket of the dark,
> To cry, 'Hold, hold!'
>
> *(I.5 39-53)*

1 Working in pairs, get the students to spend five or ten minutes reading the lines 39-53 (the entry of Macbeth). Although this is a difficult speech, the confidence gained in previous work by having experienced being able to speak Shakespeare effectively should be sufficient encouragement to tackle it. Have them sit together on the floor to read it, and move about so as to be able to respond to appeals for clarification. Incidentally, point out that Lady Macbeth's greeting to her returning husband echoes an earlier cry of the witches:

> Great Glamis! worthy Cawdor!
> Greater than both, by the *all-hail* hereafter! [my italics]

2 The students should take turns in speaking and listening. Tell them to think of Lady Macbeth as if she is trying to cast a spell with her words and her accompanying actions. Although some may find the words more difficult than others, anxiety about saying them aloud is lessened not only by the fact that only one other person is listening, but also because they are by now familiar with the informal and relaxed atmosphere of a good practical session. Encourage partners to help one another reach a tentative conclusion as to what Lady Macbeth's speech may mean at this point and, in particular, what range of movements and gestures they think might be used to accompany it.

3   After reading it together, encourage the pairs to stand and experiment with moving to the words: get one in each pair to act as a 'director' whilst the other speaks and moves. Make sure that each takes a turn in both roles.

Follow-up work

If you can, it would be useful at the completion of these exercises on the presentation of witchcraft and the supernatural or in a subsequent session on the play, to screen the extracts the students have been exploring in one of the many versions of the text now widely available on film or video. You might, for example, choose to contrast the spectacular opening of Roman Polanski's film of *Macbeth* with that of the studio-based production made by Trevor Nunn, for Independent Television, with Dame Judi Dench in the role of Lady Macbeth.

Following on from practical exploration of the text, in which students have been encouraged to look for their own meanings and how to communicate them, with a completed performance text sets up the kind of comparative analysis that stimulates thought and discussion. It also reinforces the important idea that meanings are constructed through an *active* relationship of readers and texts and that the students' own efforts are both necessary and legitimate.

Session 2

Preparation

1   Bring a candle, a jar to put it in and something to light it with.

2   Bring a cassette recorder and a pre-recorded tape of night sounds in the countryside, including, if possible the sound of an owl hooting. (See the Discography p. 116.)

Starting practical work

After warming up, distribute the text as given below.

Macbeth contains a lot of violent imagery as well as explicitly violent action. Its language too is often highly aggressive. The opening game is therefore made up of an exchange of insults taken from language used by characters in the play.

Take each person aside and whisper to him or her 'their' insult. When you have given one to everybody (some people may have the same one) set them the task of insulting one another by courtesy of Shakespeare! The game carries more weight if the behaviour of the participants is elaborately mannered in posture and gesture, and it is only in their spoken language that the veneer of civilization is stripped away.

1 If thou speak'st false,
   Upon the next tree shalt thou hang, alive,
   Till famine cling thee
2 These linen cheeks of thine
   Are counsellors to fear
3 thou lily-livered boy
4 Throw physic to the dogs!
   I'll none of it
5 Liar and slave!
6 Thou liest, thou shag-haired villain!
7 What, you egg,
   Young fry of treachery
8 We'll have thee as our rarer monsters are,
   Painted on a pole
9 An eternal curse fall on you
10 Avaunt, and quit my sight!
11 Let the earth hide thee!
12 Thy bones are marrowless, thy blood is cold
13 Hence, horrible shadow!
14 How now, you secret, black and midnight hags!
15 Thou cream-faced loon

II.1

A great deal of the action of this play takes place at night. In work that follows I want to suggest ways of exploring Macbeth's preparation for the murder of Duncan, especially by creating an atmosphere which invites students to participate fully in the 'follow-up' discussion.

1 Distribute the lines from Macbeth's speech beginning 'Is this a dagger . . .' (II .1 33) at random, one to each person.

    1 Is this a dagger which I see before me,
    2 . . . fatal vision . . .

3 . . . gouts of blood . . .
4 Nature seems dead,
5 . . . wicked dreams . . .
6 witchcraft celebrates
7 wither'd murder
8 Moves like a ghost.
9 the wolf

2 Get the whole group to sit on the floor in a circle facing inwards. Place a candle in the middle of the circle and then light it. Darken the room as much as you can. Ask the students to examine their own feelings about the night; have they any memories of frightening events that they associate with darkness? Are they still afraid of the dark?

3 Give them time to settle and then play a tape of noises recorded at night in the countryside; these should include the sound of an owl hooting. (Try the BBC sound effects tapes, see the Discography p. 116). As you will have seen earlier, you can ask the students themselves to make the appropriate noises.

4 Get the group to speak the lines at random, leaving a small pause between each speaker. As always, encourage everyone to try different ways of saying the lines. The point of this exercise, and of many like it in other sections of this book, is to create a sense of theatre that engages the emotions of the class. Once their emotional forces have been tapped, the teacher is in a much stronger position when encouraging subsequent discussion and analysis of that experience and its relationship to what happens in the play.

II.2

The next set of exercises is designed to explore further the central relationship in the play. Using text from II.2, attention is focused on what Lady Macbeth says to her husband; what it may tell us about her and what it may reveal about him.

1 Try to keep the atmosphere intact and ask the group to work in pairs. One person is to speak the lines spoken by Macbeth following Duncan's murder, the other those of his wife.

2 Distribute two photocopied sheets to the pairs with Macbeth's lines

on one and Lady Macbeth's on the other. Tell them that they are to alternate in speaking and responding. Macbeth begins. Thus:

Macbeth	Lady Macbeth
1 This is a sorry sight.	
	2 A foolish thought to say a sorry sight
3 One cried 'God bless us!'	
	4 Consider it not so deeply.
5 I could not say 'Amen'. Amen' Stuck in my throat.	
	6 These deeds must not be thought After these ways:
7 'Macbeth does murder sleep'	
	8 What do you mean?
9 'Macbeth shall sleep no more!'	
	10 You do unbend your noble strength, to think So brainsickly
11 I am afraid to think what I have done;	
	12 wash this filthy witness from your hand.
13 I'll go no more;	
	14 Infirm of purpose!
15 I dare not.	
	16 Give me the daggers.
17 every noise appals me	
	18 I shame To wear a heart so white.
19 wash this blood Clean from my hand	
	20 A little water clears us of this deed
21 they pluck out mine eyes.	

3 Judge for yourself whether it would be interesting to ask the couples one pair at a time to say their pieces whilst the rest of the group listens. If you don't have time for everybody don't ask one or two, as this encourages the kind of competition that isn't useful at this stage in the work. However, students usually like to show off their work to their peers and doing so, gives them a goal to work towards that is quite consistent with the work they have previously experienced.

For the next exercise you will be working again with larger groups.

1   Divide the class into two or three medium-sized groups – say nine in each. You are going to give them the task of speaking Lady Macbeth's thoughts after she has received and read the letter from her husband telling of his meeting with the witches. (I. 5)

2   To create a focus for the language, ask one of the group to represent Macbeth. The others should surround him or her and use these words spoken in any order and repeated several times:

> 1 thy nature . . . is too full o' the milk of human kindness
> 2 Thou wouldst be great,
> 3 Art not without ambition,
> 4 but without/The illness should attend it;
> 5 what thou wouldst highly,/That wouldst thou holily;
> 6 wouldst not play false,
> 7 yet wouldst wrongly win;
> 8 thou'dst have,/. . . That which cries, 'Thus thou must do',

3   Ask them first to say the lines in such a way as to try to persuade the figure that the speaker understands and is sympathetic to him.

4   They should then try speaking the lines as if full of impatience and anger, trying in the course of saying them to intimidate the listener.

The concluding exercise in this session first involves work in pairs and then the group as a whole working together.
    These lines will need to be memorized (at least two per student):

> 1 Was the hope drunk,/Wherein you dress'd yourself?
> 2 hath it slept since,
> 3 wakes it now,
> 4 to look so green and pale
> 5 At what it did so freely?
> 6 From this time/Such I account thy love.
> 7 Art thou afeard
> 8 To be the same in thine own act and valour/As thou art in desire?
> 9 Wouldst thou have that/Which thou esteem'st the ornament of life,
> 10 And live a coward in thine own esteem,
> 11 Letting 'I dare not' wait upon 'I would',
> 12 Like the poor cat i' the adage?
> 13 What beast was't, Then, That made you break this enterprise to me?

14 When you durst do it, then you were a man;
15 screw your courage to the sticking place,
16 What cannot you and I perform
17 we'll not fail.

(*I.7 36-61*)

In addition to their responsibility for a particular line ask all the students to also remember Macbeth's': 'If we should fail . . .

1 Working in pairs, have one partner use his or her line from the list above whilst the other is to respond with 'If we should fail . . . 'Ask them to imagine that they are trying to persuade someone to do something difficult and dangerous but at the same time exciting.

2 Get each couple to make a small working space for themselves and to experiment with different emphasis, pause, inflection and so on for five minutes or so.

3 Then they should reverse roles and repeat the exercise.

You can elaborate this exercise by asking the pairs to consider the power relationship between the two and getting them to explore ways of shifting the balance from one partner to the other. For example, get them to use a chair and to experiment with having first one partner seated and then the other. Have them try out different spatial relationships (i.e. one seated on the chair the other standing behind it or in front, kneeling etc.) Also ask the students to think about what, if any, gestures seem appropriate. Does Lady Macbeth touch her husband, hold him or hug him? What would such gestures imply about their relationship? Can this be supported by the text?

4 After some 10–15 minutes, ask the pairs to demonstrate their thinking to the group as a whole. As they do so, encourage the watching group to think of ways in which the exercise could be further elaborated. Which lines, for example, seem to require a gesture? Which lines do the group feel almost seem to require a shouted delivery, which a cajoling, wheedling voice? Individuals, or pairs if they prefer, could make their own notes on their reactions to the characters.

5 Lastly, have the whole group give a choric performance of part of Macbeth's speech from the beginning of I.7 in which he considers the magnitude of what he is about to do:

If it were done, when 'tis done,//then 'twere well
It were done quickly;//if th' assassination
Could trammel up the consequence,//and catch,

With his surcease, success;//that but this blow
Might be the be-all and the end-all// – here,
But here, upon this bank and shoal of time,//
We'd jump the life to come.//But in these cases,
We still have judgements here;//that we but teach
Bloody instructions,//which, being taught, return
To plague the inventor;//this even-handed justice
Commends the ingredients of our poison'd chalice//
To our own lips.//He's here in double trust://
First, as I am his kinsman and his subject,
Strong both against the deed;//then, as his host,
Who should against his murderer shut the door,

(I.7 1–15)

Follow-up work

Let the students take the lead, with you only taking a significant
prompting role if absolutely necessary. They should now be in a strong
position to debate and argue what kind of a relationship they think exists
between Macbeth and his wife before and immediately following Duncan's murder and make comparison with the relationship as it appears
during the rest of the action until Lady Macbeth's suicide. Someone
once described Macbeth and his wife as one of the closest married
couples in the whole of Shakespeare. What do the students make of that?

Julius Caesar

In Part 1 of this chapter we looked at how some practical exercises could
be used to create a focus on one particular character: Ophelia. Part 2
considered ways in which a group could explore supernatural elements in
Macbeth and make connections between the witches and the behaviour
of Lady Macbeth. It also looked at the changing relationship between
Macbeth and his wife as seen in the events leading up to, and
immediately following, the murder of Duncan. In this section, I want to
use a practical approach to examine not an individual but the representation by Shakespeare of the populace of Rome and especially the polit-

ical ideas about order and individual responsibility raised by the action. I hope that students following the exercises will make their own connections between the political and ethical ideas found in the text and those of Britain in the late-twentieth century.

Timing

Both sessions require a double period of 60-70 minutes.

Session 1

Preparation

1   Tell the class to bring their own copies of the text with them to the session.

2   Record on video one or two party political broadcasts for screening and subsequent analysis. If this is impractical, record from the radio or television a few minutes of a parliamentary debate, preferably illustrating at least one politician demonstrating a good rhetorical technique.

3   Re-read the opening scene of the play.

4   Obtain a pre-recorded tape of a band playing (preferably a brass band but it doesn't really matter, you just need some fairly anonymous music).

Unusually for Shakespeare, the action of this play begins with a crowd of players cluttering the stage. They are there to represent the ordinary citizens of Rome. The dialogue of two of the players (Flavius and Marullus) tells us some significant things about what Shakespeare wanted the audience to note. Although these are very ordinary working men, they are dressed not in their working clothes but in their 'best apparel', for we learn they are free from work in order to celebrate this day as a holiday in honour of Julius Caesar. The words of the two Tribunes and the responses of the citizens are the first points to examine: to see what we can learn about this society through speaking and reacting to the opening lines of the play.

Starting practical work

Begin as usual with warm-up exercises. In addition to some of those suggested in Chapter 1 (p. 20), you might consider adding the following if you have sufficient time:

1 Place three or four chairs in different parts of the room.

2 Tell the group that they are going to re-create 'Speakers' Corner'. They should think for a second or two of any subject or topic on which they feel knowledgeable, and be prepared to talk about it for one minute. It can be anything . . . the local football team, a pop band, '*Neighbours*' . . . etc.

3 Have them move around the room whilst music plays. When it stops they are to try to stand on one of the available chairs.

4 Those who succeed are now soap box orators: they must try to interest as many people as possible in their 'topic' for one minute only.

5 Start the music again and repeat the process as often as time and interest permits.

6 Distribute the following:

> 1 Hence! home, you idle creatures,
> 2 get you home.
> 3 You, sir, what trade are you?
> 4 Answer me directly.
> 5 What trade, thou knave?
> 6 thou saucy fellow!
> 7 wherefore art not in thy shop today?
> 8 You blocks,
> 9 you stones,
> 10 you worse than senseless things!
> 11 you cruel men of Rome,
> 12 Be gone!

Don't worry about the lines having to be distributed and then said in the correct order as we are not going to use choric speech for this exercise.

7 Choose three or four students to represent the citizens. Ask them to sit back-to-back in the middle of a circle formed about them by the rest of the group who stand, looking down at them.

8   Those standing should, at a signal from you, use their phrases in any order they like directed towards the seated figures.
At first everyone will probably speak at once and it won't make very much sense except to the individual speakers themselves. However, the objective at this stage is simply to get them speaking the lines and, in the process, discovering different ways of saying them.

9   After a few minutes, get the group to speak round the circle one at a time from left to right. The actual order of the printed text should still be ignored; the only important thing now is to isolate each phrase or sentence and to get the group listening to one another.

10   Once you have achieved this, ask them by using *only* their piece of text (still spoken one person at a time) to try to make the small group in the middle feel uncomfortable.

Follow-up work

When you have reached this stage, break with our more usual pattern and hold a brief 'follow-up' discussion straightaway. Have everyone sitting in a circle on the floor and ask the group, starting off with those who were seated in the middle of the circle, what impressions they had of the speakers. How do they address the people whom they represent? What sort of attitude do they appear to have? What is the tone of their speech? What, if any, particular word or phrase seems to stand out from the rest? One hopes they will pick up on the fact that the language of the Tribunes is that of people used to controlling others: indeed, the first words of the play are a directive combined with a mild insult. Get them to look out for words that are aggressive, authoritarian, confident or contemptuous. Look also at the number of questions that are fired at the citizens.

Ask everyone to look at his or her copy of the text to see how the citizens respond to this display of aggression from their social and political superiors. Point out that, essentially, the citizens are far more powerful than the Tribunes – they considerably out-number them.

To conclude this session, and following on from the discussion about how the play begins, show the party-political broadcast(s). Ask the students to try not to consider the complex issues involved but to look simply at the presentation of them by the speaker. Don't forget to use the pause button and the re-play facility from time to time in order to illustrate a particular rhetorical technique. Ask the students who, in their opinion, is making the most effective speech and why. Can the students note anything in their respective rhetorical styles that both speakers appear to have in common? Get them to pay particular attention to word repetition, emphasis and the use of pauses. How, if at all, do the speakers invite a response from their audience and when do they appear to do so? Does the pace of the speech vary etc? Ask them what, in their opinion, makes a good public speaker.

Session 2

Preparation

1 Tell the students to come to the session prepared to tell a short story or a joke. Neither must last for more than two minutes and the objective is simply to hold the attention of a group of listeners.

2 Bring an audio recording of a professional performance of *Julius Caesar* and be prepared to play the speech made by Brutus to the Plebeians after the assassination of Julius Caesar. Follow it by Mark Antony's response, III.2.

3 Make a recording of a large and quite animated crowd. Try to include sounds of laughter and excitement. (See the Discography p. 116.)

4 Tell the students to bring their own copies of the play with them to the practical session.

Starting practical work

After the warm-up introduce the following improvisation.

1 Select at random three or four 'volunteers' to tell their story or joke. Ask them where they want their 'audience' to be, whether they want them to be seated or to stand. Ask them to consider whether they will be on the same level as the audience or raised up on a box or chair?

2 Divide the group into as many parts as you have chosen speakers, and let them work together on telling the joke or story as effectively as possible. The objective is to hold the attention of an audience. And the 'audience' can offer advice or tips to the story-teller or jester. If there is some reluctance to begin or if the material doesn't seem to

work, you can always give them a text to substitute: try a well known nursery rhyme but say that it is to be spoken as if it contains a hidden coded message or tell them to speak it as if, instead of being entirely innocent, the words were the filthiest they had ever had to say in their lives.

3   Each group should spend a few minutes rehearsing together in order to make what they consider to be the most effective way of communicating the material.

4   Finally, have each group enact the speaker and 'audience' to the others.

5   Play a recording of Brutus' speech from III.2 beginning on line 13 'Romans, countrymen, and lovers!' and ending 'when it shall please my country to need my death.' (line 48). It is important that this speech and the one of Mark Antony's that follows it, are recorded onto an audio and not a video tape. You want the students to concentrate at this point on the language and how it is used by the two speakers rather than on the immediate response of the citizens. *Don't allow them to follow the text in their copies of the play.*

6   When you have played Brutus' speech, get the group to discuss how effective it was as a performance. If you play it more than once, it would be a good idea, if possible, to use recordings of two different actors. Then ask them what they remember of it: what arguments were used, what sort of language, rhetorical tricks etc were employed by Brutus?

7   Next play the recording of Mark Antony's speech beginning 'Friends, Romans, countrymen, . . .' (line 75), and go on until the end of the scene. Once again you should focus on the manner of presentation rather than just the nature of the argument in the speech. Ask the students which of the two was most affecting; which the most moving, most logical, most reasoned, most emotional, etc.

If you are short of time, there is no need to play the whole of either speech and it may help the students if you concentrate on a particular section, say the beginning and end and re-play them several times. Get the class not only listening to the rhetorical technique of the actors but also to the lines they are given to say by Shakespeare. The class must also consider carefully what it thinks are the reactions of the on-stage audience to both speakers.

The next exercise is designed to help the group explore the role of that on-stage audience of Plebians.

1   Divide the group into two roughly equal halves. Teach both a simple movement as follows.

    a   Begin standing up straight and look directly in front.

    b   Take the weight onto the left foot and step forward in a strong movement onto the right foot.

    c   As the right foot comes down, collapse the body from the waist so that the upper body and head hangs forward at the same time as the right foot hits the ground.

    d   Still keeping the body bent, draw the left foot up to be parallel with the right keeping some distance between them.

    e   As the weight is transferred to the left foot, bring the right together with it and at the same time draw the body up to its full height.

2   Once this simple step has been grasped, ask the students to add to it by clapping their hands in front of them at the point when the right foot goes down and the body collapses from the waist. Encourage the groups to synchronize this movement so that as far as possible they move as one.

3   When you first teach the step, everyone can be at a distance from each other. Once the basic step has been mastered, bring the groups together and have them practise the step, keeping as closely to one another as they can. You will find that the steps create a slow forward motion. It will take some students no time at all and others will never master it! When you have got this far make sure you put those who know what to do at the front of the group and form a wedge shape.

4   Put the two groups at opposite corners of the room, facing each other. Tell them that there must be no physical contact between them. At a signal from you, get them to move slowly towards each other. Encourage them to use eye contact with one other person from the group who is coming towards them.

5   As the groups approach the centre of the space, the movement and clapping should become progressively stronger and louder. At the time when the front players in the 'wedge' meet, the sound should be at its height. In fact you can add to it by using the recording of

crowd noise, gradually increasing the volume to match and augment the noises made by the two rival groups.

6   Get the individuals in both groups to separate sufficiently to enable them to pass through one another and thus move on to occupy the opposite corner of the room from that in which they started. As they pass one another and move again into open space, so the intensity of the movement, the sound of the clapping and the taped noises should diminish and, by the time the groups have reached their destinations, the space, the sound and movement should be minimal.

The exercise is, in musical terms, an attempt to make a crescendo as the two groups come together and then a diminuendo as they separate and pass. Although it may sound complicated, it isn't in practice, and you can in any case make your own variant of it. It is, however, very useful especially when what you require involves ritualized movement.

Encourage each group to behave as a single unit. Once their movements are reasonably disciplined, you should instruct them to think aggressively about the other group. Their movements and eye contact should form a physical attempt to intimidate the others. They should try to out-clap, out-stamp, and out-face them. The only rule is that there is *no* physical contact.

7   Following on from this exercise it would be useful and appropriate to sit down together and briefly discuss what it felt like to be part of a group moving and behaving as one. Did people feel aggressive/excited/angry? This is an obvious opening for talking and thinking about group behaviour and how individuals behave in groups as opposed to when they are alone or in twos and threes. The idea of group pressure could be discussed and the issue of individual responsibility . . . does it become more difficult to exercise restraint when part of a larger group, and, if so, why? Introduce the question of how groups of individuals are influenced. What makes a group respond (e.g. in football violence, anger on picket lines, mass meetings, 'pop' concerts, group intimidation in the playground and so on).

8   Get the group to sit down and look at their copies of the play and read aloud (or follow the voices of the actors in the recording) III.3. Here we see precisely what Mark Antony's speech that we heard in the previous exercise has moved the citizens towards: an uncontrolled violent mob who will kill an innocent man simply because his name happens to

correspond to that of one of the assassins of Julius Caesar. The group have also *experienced* something of what it feels like to be a part of a mob.

9   To conclude, play the whole of this sequence from the BBC production of *Julius Caesar*, starting from the speech made by Brutus in III.3 up to and including the exit of the mob at the end of III.3.

Follow-up work

Take the speeches of Brutus and Mark Antony in III.2 (or extracts from them) and make a photocopy of them from your own text of the play. Tippex out all the punctuation (some of it will still be obvious because you should leave any capital letters) and set the students the task of creating their own punctuation. However, stress that this punctuation is designed not for a reader, but as an *aide memoire* for a public speaker. Therefore, not only should the speech be punctuated but also an indication given of the length of any pauses, where a particular word or phrase is to be emphasized. Encourage them to include a note of any accompanying gestures of hands or eyes which might be used to emphasize a particular point or to draw attention to the speaker at an especially important moment in his peroration. Such a piece of work could of course be included as part of a unit of work in a GCSE folder.

In a future practical session on the play, you could make further use of this material by having members of the group read out extracts from 'their' speeches and discuss the impact of them on the audience. You could, if you wish, re-create the soap-box improvisation, having the speakers speaking some of the Brutus or Mark Antony text, whilst their listeners use the lines spoken by the tribunes and used in Session 1 to try to punctuate the rhetoric like hecklers in Hyde Park. You could also lead a discussion on audience reaction.

4

Walking Through

Thus far in this book a lot of attention has been paid to practical work that uses choric speech and games as its main method of exploring plays by Shakespeare. This chapter outlines an alternative, but still practical, approach to teaching Shakespeare. The teaching method described could be undertaken in a classroom where desks and chairs have been pushed back to create an open space. In 'walking through' a scene or part of a scene, the students are working in a way which follows on from work described in Chapters 2 (p. 30) and 3 (p. 67) and the broad objectives remain the same: to stimulate interest and curiosity in Shakespeare through an immediate and personal experience of his work. Although I have chosen a scene from *Macbeth* (III.4) the 'banquet scene', as an example of the range of interpretative issues potentially thrown up by working in this way, my objective is to demonstrate a method of working that could be applied to *any* Shakespeare play, or indeed to most examples of dramatic literature.

Active reading

In following the work outlined in this chapter the student ought to experience what I choose to call active reading. Although most if not all of the issues explored in the subsequent dramatic analysis of the scene are accessible to a student simply reading the text very carefully, this is a difficult task for a young reader. When that reader picks up a dramatic text and begins to read she or he inevitably begins to imagine the action taking place in the theatre of the mind's eye. The process of 'walking through' encourages and schools the dramatic imagination, helping the reader become more aware of theatrical conventions and the role they play in the construction of meanings in performance. Walking through should also help to crystallize the action, it becomes a *'thing done'*, and if a student has participated in seeing how meanings can be made and unmade, then she or he is in a strong position to make critical judgements about the real or imagined page-to-stage process.

As I have argued and demonstrated in previous chapters, a basically simple choric method that gets young people actively and expressively speaking a text from the beginning stands a good chance of getting over the potentially enormous barrier posed by archaic language. However, teachers working at 'A' level and post–'A' level, and those with able GCSE pupils may find the method on its own too limited, when what they require is a more detailed analytical approach. 'Walking through' creates a climate favourable to close textual study whilst at the same time not jettisoning the active intellectual and emotional involvement of the students themselves. In my experience it works best when used as a follow-up to choric speech and not as a more 'academic' substitute for it.

Basically 'walking through' mirrors a rehearsal technique. The teacher is in the role of the stage director and the class that of performers and audience. At first that may not appear to be a desirable pedagogical model: the teacher should not direct the class what to think. However, that relationship should not be taken to imply that in this context the teacher is directing students towards his or her own reading of the text but, like a good theatre director, he or she will encourage the actors-students by prompting them to make their own discoveries about the text.

This way of working, like the other approaches outlined previously, does not have to *remain* teacher-centred. The role of the teacher is to organize a structured introduction to this practical way of working on a text that promotes confidence, and demonstrably opens-up important critical questions. Once sufficient confidence and elementary procedural knowledge has been transferred to the students, they can begin to assume responsibility for their own learning. A large class can be broken-down into smaller groups and the role of director taken by a student or it can be shared by the group as a whole. Indeed, it is always desirable at some stage to introduce collective decision-making because it invariably provokes a useful debate concerning textual authority, and the interpretative role of the director *vs* that of the actor, audience, reader etc.

As in the previous work, the objective is not to create individual performances but to explore collectively issues and ideas that only become obvious once questions relevant to performers (and audiences) are raised. The students will spend most of their time on their feet, but the role of the teacher is to make them *think* on their feet.

Using a printed text

Unlike choric work, at least some of the class will need access to a printed text for some of the time. Although it involves extra work for the teacher, and extra expense for the school, I strongly recommend that for this particular form of practical work the students are only given a printed sheet(s) with the relevant text copied onto it rather than trying to work from the full published version of the play.

I recommend this for two main reasons. Firstly, the sheet of paper or file card is easier to handle, it won't get in the way of movement and gesture to the extent that a printed book might. Secondly, and more importantly, it is psychologically much easier for the student to handle. Transposing the text from the printed version into one that is hand-written or typed and then photocopied, lends a much more temporary, unfinished and therefore less authoritative air to the text. Of course, any text by Shakespeare or any other dramatist (or a novel or a poem) *is* incomplete and partial until the dimension brought to it by the reader has been added. In the case of dramatic literature, the objective is very much to encourage the *active* reading of students, and therefore they must start by acknowledging that their text is incomplete and that, in order to complete it for themselves, much interpretative work remains to be done. Therefore the less 'authoritative' and awe inspiring the printed text appears the better: it almost needs to look rough and unfinished.

Casting

In 'walking through', the class will be required to consider the printed text of the play both from the perspective of actors and that of spectators. The session is not a rehearsal for a performance, but an attempt to discover how meanings are constructed. As part of the preparation for this work, the teacher must cast some individuals in particular roles, something we avoided in choric work. Those whose task it is actually to read a text as part of the exercise will obviously need to be prepared and, if it is a long extract, forewarned. But, although some of the participants will superficially appear to have more to do than others, if the teaching situation is handled with care it will soon become apparent that each member of the group has a role to play in determining the range of meanings contained within the extract selected for practical study.

The class as audience

At times during a 'walk through' it is useful to use some of the class as 'audience' *if*, that is, using them in that way ensures that they are as active as those enacting the text. For example, in soliloquy, is the actor to talk *to* them, or to ignore them? What difference does it make? When using 'asides', how are they to be delivered?

If the audience of students is continually encouraged to be constructively critical of the work of their peers, then their comments and reactions can help shape the interpretation of the performers. From their position of relative objectivity, they, together with the teacher-director, can also usefully draw attention to the whole question of theatrical conventions both of the Elizabethan/Jacobean theatre and those of theatre in Britain in the late twentieth century. By using students as both performers and audience it will soon become apparent that the 'text' is not simply what actors *say*, nor what they *do*, but that text is created through the interaction of actors and audiences. When using some of the group as an audience, it is very important indeed that:

> it is not always the same group who get to watch, and the period they are expected to sit still and concentrate does not exceed 10 minutes.

> they are aware that their task is to watch, listen, and comment.

Unless the teacher prevents it, the 'audience' group will tend at first to have their heads down in their copies of the play following the words as they are spoken. Try to ensure that they are concentrating on what they see and hear on stage.

Objectives

General

- **To encourage** students to use their eyes as well as their ears when 'reading' a scene.

- **To encourage** them to prepare for a practical class by bringing ideas of their own to try out and test, and not to rely solely on their peers and especially not on the teacher.

- **To recognize** that the cooperative pooling of ideas is a necessary part of any presentational strategy, and a wholly legitimate part of exploring the process of making texts into performances.

- **To encourage** a more thoughtful and thorough approach to the language of Shakespeare by speaking and listening to it and, above all, by creating a dramatic context in which that language is heard and understood.

Specific

The shape of a scene To discuss the potential significance of exits and entrances and all movements on the playing space. How many characters are on stage at any one time? Can their movements onto and off the playing space be recorded and if so, what patterns emerge?

Location Where is the action set and how does an audience know? Does the location change? If so, when and why and how? Is the action taking place inside or outside? How do the audience know? Is it of any significance either way?

Time How is the passing of stage time signalled to the audience? (I .1 of *Hamlet*, for example, goes from just before midnight to shortly after dawn.) Does the time of day or year change to any great extent during the action?

Character identification How do we know who is speaking and what his or her relationship is to his or her on-stage listeners? How do we know what we know about them: e.g. class, age, status, occupation?

Properties What properties are required by the text (Desdemona's handkerchief for example, or Yorick's skull)? How are they used? Can the choice of certain properties affect the way in which the action is understood? For example, in the banquet scene in *Macbeth* what difference does it make if the table is set with elaborate and expensive china and glass, or set with crude wooden bowls, and knives for hacking at the meat? Can an argument be made for the choice of a particular property?

Costume What indication is there, if any, in the text spoken by the actors of what a character wears? Does this change during the action? How is costume used to suggest things about characters and to reinforce ideas in the play as a whole? For example, King Lear's mental disintegration from a powerful but irascible King to a mad, defenceless beggar is mirrored in his costume which changes from riches to rags. Or in the banquet scene in *Macbeth* if Lady Macbeth is shown wearing a glorious rich gown indicating her material ambitions have been realized, a tremendous contrast can be effected the next time she is seen. In the famous 'sleep-walking scene' (V.1) she is wearing a nightgown, the symbols of her material power have been removed, and in her dream-like state she appears vulnerable, revealing to the astonished Doctor and Gentlewoman, the hidden fears of her conscience.

Gesture Is there any indication in the text of a particular gesture made by a character? For instance, 'Leave wringing of your hands' (Hamlet to Gertrude, II.4, 35); or, when 'walking through', does the action seem to call for one? For example a bow, an embrace, a kiss.

Silent characters To note which of the characters 'on-stage' are speaking the text, and to decide which, by listening and watching, are also engaged in making meaning. To acknowledge, therefore, that listening is an expressive act. As we will see in the work to be undertaken on the banquet scene (III.4) in *Macbeth*, we need to be alive to the possibilities for using actors who, although they have no actual words to speak, can nonetheless contribute in significant ways to the construction of meanings.

Theatrical fidelity To discuss the status of the printed text and its relation to what is performed. To explore the possible range of meanings contained within a text and to consider at what point interpretation becomes adaptation.

A classroom-based rehearsal

Preparation

1 Read III.4 of *Macbeth* bearing in mind the objectives just outlined.

2 Clear the space of as many obstacles to free movement as possible. Decide how much of the space is to be occupied by the 'audience'; how much allocated to the performers. Even if all the students are to be involved as performers it is important that they acknowledge that, on some level, what they are doing is designed to be communicated to an audience.

3 In consultation with the group, decide how large the playing space is going to be. Consider whether there are any separate levels within it

(e.g. a balcony or raised space made by rostra or tables); where the exits and entrances are sited and where the audience is in relation to the actors.

If you are working with sixth formers they might, for example, look at what is known of the original playing conditions in the Elizabethan public theatre. Two books that every school library ought to have will help in this research:

Andrew Gurr: *The Shakespearean Stage 1574-1642,* Cambridge University Press, 1982.

Peter Thomson: *Shakespeare's Theatre,* Routledge & Kegan Paul, 1983.

Both authors write in a clear and entertaining way that will open up this complex field of scholarly research to a student readership and also, and importantly, establish a connection in the minds of the students themselves between academic and practical work: the one informing the other in an active way. Young people will find Thompson's book particularly accessible, and his chapter *'Macbeth* from the tiring house', would be very useful indeed read alongside the material in this chapter.

4   Once practical decisions have been taken, if possible mark out the dimensions of the area on the floor with chalk or masking tape and place chairs or cushions where the audience are meant to be. It is important to make the *playing* space as concrete as possible. Having said that, avoid using an actual raised stage (like the one usually found in the school hall). Purpose-built theatre spaces carry with them too many of the wrong associations, usually connected with inappropriate naturalistic performance conventions and also may raise false expectations about the nature of this kind of work which must be *process* and not *product* orientated.

5   The second part of the collective preparation involves reading the scene. If this work comes after some experience of the 'choric' approach it may now prove less problematic than before to get the class to read aloud. It is necessary to read the scene together if only to establish, at this stage, the sequence of the action within it. If the reading will require one or two individuals in relatively lengthy passages, it will obviously help smooth the process if they are given adequate advance notice and can come to you for help and advice if they need it.

One simple alternative to having the class read is to hand the reading over to professional actors. Play a recording of the scene made by professional actors and have the class follow the text in their own editions of the play. However, some young people do display a real talent for expressive reading and it would seem a pity not to afford them the opportunity of displaying it, providing always it is in a context where other students recognize that they also have active and *equally* important roles to play.

6   Once the printed text has been spoken and decisions made on the shape and area of the 'stage', then, initially adopting the role of director yourself, bring the 'actors' onto it and begin walking through.

Experience will teach you how often to stop the action in order to ask a question, and when to let it go on without interruption. Ideally the students themselves will want to keep stopping in order to discuss the position of an actor(s), the need for a gesture, etc. In a 'walk-through' there will sometimes be a number of students watching and listening. Make sure that it isn't the same people all the time. Ideally everyone should have to experience the scene from the point of view not only of its leading players but also from that of the audience and also the so-called minor characters (who may be of major dramatic significance). Above all avoid the exercise turning into a performance in which one or two 'actors' are doing the majority of the interpretative work whilst the rest of the group remain passive consumers.

I have outlined above the general preparation that, for the most part, the class can undertake together. However, as in the majority of teaching exercises, the success or otherwise of the project is to a large extent dependent upon the quality of the *teacher's* preparation that goes into it. Unlike previous practical sessions, I offer no lesson plan for this work. Instead, what I propose to do is to analyse a specific scene as if I were preparing myself to teach it to an 'A' level class. The objective here is to establish a *method* of work, and this kind of preparation is an important part of that method. I draw attention to particular interpretative and perhaps contentious issues in staging. These are the kind of areas that I hope 'walking through' III.4 of *Macbeth* would target. Of course, this is *a* reading of the scene and certainly has no claim to be 'authoritative'. It simply illustrates some of the interpretative issues with which *I* would want a group 'walking through' this scene to engage critically.

What most teachers of English will immediately note when they read my analysis is the lack of specific attention given to Shakespeare's language. There is no discussion of imagery, plot or character. This is not meant to indicate that they are unimportant in a study of Shakespeare: close study of them is a vital part of any public sector examination. However, language when it is spoken and heard in a theatre is understood by an audience in a specific dramatic context: a context manufactured by a combination of all the elements of the production. 'Walking through' demands that students consider that dramatic context in which the spoken language of the actors is only one of the possible channels of communication. The broad objective behind 'walking through' is not only to encourage students to think, for example, of how visual metaphors are made, but also to get them to recognize that meanings are made in a variety of inter-related ways, and are fluid rather than fixed. *Their* contribution to the work can be demonstrated as significant, and therefore exciting and challenging.

Text into performance

When *Macbeth* was first performed by the Lord Chamberlains's men in 1606, it was almost certainly an audience in the Globe theatre on Bankside which was lucky enough to see it. The Globe, of course, was a theatre open to the elements and performances there took place in daylight. Therefore, if action taking place at 'night' needed to be established on stage, this had to be achieved through the words and gestures of the actors and by the use of specific stage properties such as torches. There are plenty of scenes in other plays by Shakespeare and his contemporaries that contain scenes which take place at night, but few plays of this period require so much of their action to occur under cover of darkness as does *Macbeth*.

> . . . Come, seeling night,
> Scarf up the tender eye of pitiful day,
> And with thy bloody and invisible hand
> Cancel and tear to pieces that great bond
> Which keeps me pale! Light thickens, and the crow
> Makes wings to the rooky wood;
> Good things of day begin to droop and drowse,
> Whiles night's black agents to their preys do rouse.
> *(III.2 46-53)*

The scene which forms the basis of this dramatic analysis and my preparation for a subsequent 'walking through' exercise takes place at night. The preceding scene (III.3) is short, violent, chaotic, and bloody. Murderers – 'night's black agents' – who are often played in contemporary performances by actors recognizable as those who also take the parts of the three witches, ambush Banquo and Fleance. The latter escapes. With torches and a spoken reference ('The west yet glimmers with some streaks of day'), the text makes a particular point of signalling that the action in III.3 is taking place in semi-darkness. Establishing through these conventions that it is dark facilitated the credibility of the plot: allowing Fleance to escape. But the main function of darkness is metaphoric. These killers are acting on behalf of the new King of Scotland whose deeds must needs be done in darkness and in secret. Duncan was killed at night as he slept and here the darkness covering the gross act of Banquo's murder is itself symbolic of the dark reign of Macbeth, underpinned by assassinations and intrigue.

The action of the banquet scene also takes place at night and though it appears to be a total contrast to what has immediately preceded it, there are continual reminders in the action which drag the audience and Macbeth away from the glittering world of state, characterized by formal elaborate rituals, back to a harsher, cruder world characterized by violent anarchic action in which innocent men are slaughtered. The scene is set for a state banquet at which all those of rank and distinction in Scotland (except Banquo) are present. It is reasonable to surmise that the occasion is formal: the meal is the first opportunity for the new King and his Queen to entertain the nobility of Scotland, and thus, through the shared fellowship of the meal, symbolically to unite the kingdom under its new King. In performance, costumes could perhaps be chosen to emphasize both the nature of the occasion, and the rank of those wearing them. The entrance of the characters should be formal; perhaps accompanied by music, each entering according to the precedence to which his rank entitles him.

Macbeth's first words tell us that the seating at table is also, as convention dictated on ceremonial occasions, according to the etiquette of state:

> You know your own degrees; sit down: . . .

There is an ironic undertone to this speech, for while all the invited guests do indeed know their own degrees, Macbeth knows his to be illegitimate. All the guests are then seated. In the first performances of this play it is likely that the seats of the King and Queen were distinguished in some way from the others, perhaps by a ceremonial canopy. Certainly, they would have been seated in prominent positions at the table. However, Macbeth does not immediately sit down. In fact, he is on his feet for the whole of this scene and is never seen as being united with or heading his countrymen. As the Lords are presumably settling into their seats, he moves around the table in order to

> mingle with society/And play the humble host

But as we know, Macbeth greatly abused his role of host when he 'entertained' Duncan at his house. Moreover, as the preceding scene makes clear, this man indeed 'plays' the humble host rather than showing his true murderous self. As he moves around, perhaps greeting his guests, the most important seat at the table is vacant. Symbolically this is powerful, because Macbeth is not the legitimate King of Scotland and is therefore unfit to preside at a state occasion.

Lady Macbeth remains seated and, together with the rest of the company, waits to begin eating. Before Macbeth can join them, and the meal commence, the potential for a harmonious image is shattered when Macbeth's attention is drawn to the presence of a figure standing apart from the company, whose face is smeared with blood. The sight of the 'bloody man' serves to trigger the audience's visual memory, connecting them not only to the previous scene but to a whole series of bloody images left in the wake of the preceding action: the bloody hands of Macbeth after the killing of Duncan, the killing of Banquo and the first terrible image of blood encountered by the court of Duncan after the witches have left the stage (I.1) and the startled King cries out:

> What bloody man is that?

With the entrance of the figure of the murderer, the audience sees both the spectacle of a state banquet and a lone, blood-smeared figure: a grossly incongruous and even grotesque juxtaposing of images. The dramatic consequence of this is that, even now, when Macbeth should be revelling in his newly acquired power, his preoccupation is not with his country's leaders and nobles but with its dregs, through whose agency he attempts to sustain his authority.

Macbeth's speech, as he moves quickly to confront the uninvited guest, is in contrast to that he has so recently employed upon his other guests. From:

> Be large in mirth; anon, we'll drink a measure
> The table round.

He moves immediately to:

> There's blood upon thy face.

The audience watches simultaneously the guests and the Queen, seated at the table laden with food and drink, and Macbeth, who is deeply engaged with the murderer of Banquo. He praises his villainy warmly:

>   Thou art the best o' the cut-throats; . . .

Anyone staging this scene, either in the theatre or in the imagination, has to decide what the seated players are doing whilst Macbeth and the murderer are deep in conversation. It would seem important to the meaning of the scene as a whole that they do not begin to eat or drink. Protocol dictates that they wait for the King. If they are seen to be waiting, perhaps rather awkwardly passing the time in conversation with one another, it shows the audience that this event, which ought to symbolize Macbeth's legitimacy, is never concluded; instead of a triumphant demonstration of the new King's hospitality and generosity, the evening degenerates into a fiasco. Order is transformed into disorder. The food remains uneaten, the wine untasted.

After the exit of the murderer, Macbeth's mind is already distracted from the ceremony he so confidently began minutes before. The failure to dispose of Fleance has fractured the temporary elation he experienced when hearing the news of the death of Banquo. Murder, not the ceremony and pleasures of kingship, is his preoccupation now:

>   . . . I am cabin'd, cribb'd, confin'd, bound in
>   To saucy doubts and fears.

Lady Macbeth has to call him back to his role of host (and King):

>   My *royal* Lord,
>   You do not give the cheer: . . . (my italics)

Lennox invites Macbeth to sit, join in the company and make the table harmonious. But before he can do so, Banquo's ghost enters and sits in his place, disrupting the spectacle. Those around the table cannot see the figure but Macbeth and the audience can. The image of blood on the face of the murderer has now developed into the image of a murdered man covered in blood:

>   . . . never shake
>   Thy gory locks at me.

The response of Macbeth to the apparition understandably perplexes and further unsettles the Lords. Ross suggests to the others that the meal cannot continue:

>   Gentlemen, rise; his highness is not well.

But Lady Macbeth quickly intervenes with a contrary instruction:

>   Sit, worthy friends:

For the second time in the scene she has seen her role as being the one who attempts to hold together the unity of the occasion. The Lords obviously don't know how to react to this extraordinary interruption of a familiar state ritual. Lady Macbeth has again to insist:

> . . . pray you, keep seat; . . .

before the company reluctantly comply. Leaving their Monarch still standing and isolated from the rest of the company, she gives an instruction to the men to:

> Feed, and regard him not . . .

whilst, presumably, she also leaves the table to confront her husband. We now have the banquet with neither host nor hostess present. In such circumstances eating the meal would have been unthinkable. The Lords are left stranded, unable to continue the ritual without the main players and unsure of what course of action to take.

Lady Macbeth's anger and frustration with her husband come because she thinks that he is imagining that the figure of Duncan is present. She has no knowledge of the killing of Banquo and attacks Macbeth's behaviour by comparing it to that prior to the act of regicide:

> O proper stuff!
> This is the very painting of your fear;
> This is the air-drawn dagger which, you said,
> Led you to Duncan.

It is apparently the increasingly obvious fascination and horror of the guests that compels Macbeth eventually to listen to the promptings of his wife and return to the table. He calls for wine and is about to drink a toast when Banquo's ghost re-enters. The timing of the entrance coincides with the toast from King to subjects; the chorus that returns their sovereigns good wishes is seemingly and inexplicably followed by an insult:

> Avaunt! and quit my sight!

The guests soon realize that Macbeth is not addressing them but still have no clear idea of who or what is causing this behaviour. Unlike the first appearance of the ghost, there is no recovering the situation after his second showing. When their curiosity spills over into interrogation, Lady Macbeth is quick to insist, not that they remain seated but that they go, and go quickly:

> At once, good night:

> Stand not upon the order of your going,
> But go at once.

This banquet which began so formally with due regard paid to status and appropriate behaviour, ends in chaos and disarray as the order symbolized in the etiquette of state is disregarded in the hurried exit from the room. Macbeth has disgraced himself both in front of those whose superior he now affects to be and also in front of the servants, the attendants at the meal whose lives are governed by such as those gathered round this table. Aside from the evidence of his involvement in something distinctly unsavoury, the assembled nobility of Scotland might well leave the table with considerable misgivings as to the fitness of this man (whose wife has just described as having a chronic condition) to hold the highest office in the land.

The ending of the scene has Macbeth looking towards a meeting with the three witches and to the next murder. Lady Macbeth, once his partner in ambition, is now distanced from him. She is ignorant of the web he is weaving, a web which will eventually entrap them both. The only way in which she can now respond is to suggest that what Macbeth needs is sleep:

> You lack the season of all natures, sleep.

The scene ends with Macbeth leading his wife off stage in search of comforting sleep. But calm and trouble-free rest are not to be enjoyed by either of this couple. The 'sleep that sometimes shutteth sorrows eyes' is denied them. They cannot escape the guilt of what they have done.

Further notes on interpreting the play

The notes that follow are intended as a further guide to the kind of interpretative issues (specifically concerning this scene) that I would hope would be thrown up in the process of 'walking it through'.

Macbeth, III.4

1 **Setting** How do we know that it is dark? How soon in the action of the scene does the spoken language indicate the time of day? The actors, of course, could signal darkness by carrying lighted torches. If it is possible, try to explore the action in semi-darkness. If you can

use candle light, the shadows cast will prove a good talking point for a lot of the play's imagery as well as providing areas of relative darkness and light on-stage.

2 **Characters** Who is present in this scene apart from the named characters? What role do they collectively play? How do they behave? Is their behaviour 'formal' or 'informal', and what do those terms mean? What meanings are opened up (and closed down)? Is the behaviour of some of the Lords rough, even loutish? Do they display a different code of behaviour from that of others (e.g. servants) also involved in the scene?

How will you use the servants? Obviously they have to wait on the table, but do you want to use them to make a political point? Are they cowed and under-fed, representing for the audience a people starving in a Scotland neglected by its new king and his followers? Do you want to reinforce this political reading by supplying one or two armed guards on the entrances and exits to the room to signal that this is a king who is constantly on guard against potential assassins? Will there be a performer whose role is to enact a 'taster' to the food to check that no one is trying to poison the nobility and especially the King?

3 **Status** Try out some exercises that require individuals to manifest in their behaviour differences in social status. For example, working in twos, ask the group to improvise a simple social occasion such as a tea party. In the process of giving and receiving the tea one of the 'hosts' should attempt (whilst always remaining polite) to assert a higher status than that of their guest. Discuss with the group the difference between public and private, formal and informal behaviour.

4 **The banquet** Discuss the banquet in contemporary terms. For example, a visit to the UK by a Head of State from a neighbouring country and the subsequent formal welcome at, say, Buckingham Palace or Number 10 Downing Street. Who would sit where? What would the participants wear: medals, jewels, uniforms, honours/ insignia etc. Alternatively, is the scene a domestic one in which the Macbeths entertain friends at home? If so, what difference would this make to the overall meanings of the action? How formal or informal is this gathering? Are other wives present? Do you want to signal a sense of unease amongst the guests? Is there already speculation about the death of Duncan whilst under Macbeth's roof? Or, are the guests relaxed and comfortable, either because they don't know (and don't care) about the circumstances that brought Macbeth to power,

or because they may know but are corrupt: interested only in power, not in whether it is legitimately held?

5   **Entrances** Get the group to try out different entrances. Who comes in first? The table and chairs would presumably have to be 'set' by the servants perhaps? How are they preparing for the entry of the guests? Do the audience hear the arrival before they witness it? Is there to be a musical cue on entry (i.e. a 'flourish' or is the first sound the noisy and excited talking of the guests)? Are Macbeth and Lady Macbeth together, or, as in modern state banquets, does each accompany the appropriate gender of the visiting dignitaries?

6   **Timing** Timing is important. How long do you give it before Macbeth speaks the opening lines? How long is the pause after the instruction to 'sit down'? Following the exit of the assassins, is there a pause before Lady Macbeth calls her husband back to his role of host? If so, how long should the pause be and what effect will it achieve?

Explore the *timing* of the reactions of the lords to Macbeth's behaviour and to the contrary set of instructions issuing from the King and Queen. Discuss the potential significance of the fact that control and the role of host are being transferred from a man to, presumably, the only woman present.

7   **Relationships** Get all of the performers to think about their roles and to discover at least one distinctive action that makes a statement about how they see that role: for example, if playing a servant, what gesture should be made upon the entrance of the new King of Scotland? If playing an unnamed Lord, is the relationship to other Lords present friendly or suspicious and how should this be signalled to an audience?

8   **The hierarchy** What *is* the order of their 'own degrees'? Do they know what it is and, more importantly, are they to be seen as implicitly accepting that degree or has Macbeth's ambition to advance his own degree sowed the seed of ambition in others? To whom does Macbeth go first? To the Lord with the most seniority? How does he 'play' the humble host?

9   **The King and Queen** Where are the places reserved for Macbeth and Lady Macbeth? Where would their seats be placed and why? Again you could draw attention to contemporary practice; for instance in the Cabinet room, who sits where in relation to the Prime Minister? When negotiating the Strategic Arms Limitation Talks

between Russia and America who sits where and why is it significant?

10 **Macbeth** Will the audience be aware of the fact that he is 'role playing'? How can it be emphasized?

11 **Lady Macbeth** Does anyone talk to Lady Macbeth? How does she behave? What does the performer in the role want to signal: triumph at achieving the summit of her ambition? Pride? A growing sense that she is becoming isolated from her husband? At what point, does Lady Macbeth leave the table? Where are the couple now standing in relation to the other players? Are they static or moving? What is the reaction of the servants to the behaviour of their masters? How should Lady Macbeth respond to the actions of her husband? She has been under great stress. Is she angry/gentle/consoling etc? How do Lady Macbeth and her husband exit . . . arms around one another. . . separately as if estranged by the experience?

12 **The murderer** How will the focus of attention be drawn to the figure of the murderer? Is it by what Macbeth says here or earlier in the action? Does he come in unnoticed with the guests? What does he look like? Is he dressed differently from the Lords? Is it of any possible significance if the murderer is dressed as a servant?

13 **The guests** During Macbeth's conversation with the murderer, what is happening at the table? It is a long wait for the guests; do they begin to signal unease at the absence of their host? How does Lady Macbeth cope? What balance will you strike between creating a focus on Macbeth and on his guests? Do they attempt to ignore what is happening? Do some display a marked (and growing) curiosity? (The reaction of Ross signals that at least some of the guests have overheard at least part of what Macbeth has been saying.) At what point should it become obvious to the audience that this is what has happened? How much has been overheard?

How is this exit to be staged? Do they all 'go quickly'? Do some linger to stare at Macbeth? How long does it take to clear the stage? Once the stage is left to Macbeth and Lady Macbeth how should it appear to the audience? An abandoned banquet . . . food untouched . . . spilt wine . . . a scene of confusion in contrast to the order with which the action began?

14 **The ghost** Will Banquo's ghost be physically represented or not? If the answer is 'yes', from where will he enter and at what stage in the

action? Could he be present from the beginning, hidden amongst the servants?

15 **Silent characters** How might you use some of the players if you wanted to add a further political dimension to the action? What reading of the scene would be strengthened if, for example, on the exit of the King and Queen one or two servants emerge from hiding and, laughing heartily, begin to complete the incomplete ceremony of the meal?

Follow-up work

1 Ask the students to put themselves in the position of a guest at this banquet. They have to write a letter to close friends in which they describe the events and, importantly, say what they think lies behind them.

Take time to encourage individuals in the group to read their letters to the others and encourage a discussion of what was or was not observed. Just as the students have shared in the construction of a reading of the banquet scene, encourage them to share their discoveries with one another, to become readers of each other's writing.

2 Rewrite the scene in modern colloquial English as if it were a chapter in a novel.

3 Make notes based on observations of the qualities and effects of Shakespeare's language in this scene. Note which words seem particularly significant; which words (adjectives in particular) are repeated.

4 Consider one of the following roles: Macbeth, Lady Macbeth, or the murderer, and go through his or her speeches carefully, looking at where an actor might lay a particular stress or emphasis on a word or phrase. Also look at the punctuation in the modern script and consider whether, again thinking as an actor, the student might wish to modify it. Look particularly hard at where a pause might come.

5 If some students express a particular interest in stage-design, get them to make drawings of how they would set the banquet scene. You could specify a historical period (say late-twentieth century), and ask them to illustrate the room, its furnishings and fittings plus one or two designs for costumes to be worn by the principal characters and those in minor roles.

In doing this work, the students would have to think both in terms of the creation of visual metaphors, and about the issues of class, status and power raised by the preceding walk through. The illustrations should be accompanied by a written file that argues for the visual interpretation represented in the drawings.

Written work

In this work, and indeed in all of the practical approaches advocated in the whole of the book, students working at all levels can usefully be asked to keep a *personal note book* or *journal* recording their work on a text. Indeed, for GCSE this could provide the primary written task: a lesson by lesson, or week by week record of what they did.

Teachers would need to allow time each week for their students to talk over the activities and to make notes. Perhaps some of the time allocated to homework could be used in writing up the notes fully and neatly. All students, from GCSE to undergraduates would need to be frequently reminded to do this and given opportunities to record their observations, discoveries and reactions before their memories begin to erase the experience. A number of headings might be placed in the front of the notebook or journal to remind the students of the things they should record, namely:

Personal involvement:
What they did, thought and learnt when coping with the various practical exercises.

Record of the plot:
A brief account of each stage in the unfolding narrative.

Record of more general discussions:
For example, what was revealed about a certain character during work on a specific scene; the dramatic tension between characters; the atmosphere of a scene and how it was created.

Observations on Shakespeare's language:
Make lists of particular kinds of words:
e.g. 'aggressive' words; 'soft'/'gentle' words; words connected with money; business; blood; darkness; ceremony; animals, etc.
Record any words whose meaning remains unclear with an attempt to state what the word might mean in a particular context.
Make lists of recurrent words or phrases: for example those used as greetings, insults etc.

Postscript

Stage directions

Many scholarly editions of Shakespeare's plays refer in the notes or the introduction somewhat disparagingly to 'stage business'. But that 'business' (i.e. the movements, gestures, actions that arise out of the creative work of actors and directors in rehearsal) is largely what this chapter is about. Many readers of plays get their information about such business from the stage directions, and use is made of them in this work. However, it is important to be reminded that the authority of those directions in plays by Shakespeare (or by most other Elizabethan and Jacobean dramatists) is ultimately editorial not authorial.

There is no manuscript surviving of a play by Shakespeare. The stage directions, like the text itself, are drawn by modern editors from quartos and folios published either when Shakespeare was still alive or, as in the case of the first folio, posthumously. These directions only provide possible indications of Elizabethan playhouse conventions and should be treated as guidelines rather than rules as to how to 'read' a scene. For example, a stage direction indicating the entrance of a group of characters such as that for I.2 of *Hamlet*:

> *Flourish. Enter Claudius, King of Denmark, Gertrude the Queen, and the Council, including Polonius with his son Laertes, Hamlet, Voltemand, Cornelius, and attendants*

may *exclude* others (notably Ophelia) not for interpretative reasons but because in the first productions of the play, the actor playing the role was required to represent someone else at the time. There is nothing in the subsequent spoken text to indicate that Ophelia is *not* present in this crucial early scene, and her presence would be an opportunity for some interesting stage 'business'.

This direction, like many others, is also vague about the numbers of players required for the specific scene. It refers only to named characters and, in this case, to the Council and attendants. The permanent Elizabethan company of actors numbered no more than about ten to twelve; 'hired men' were drafted in to fill the extra roles as required. But these roles, 'attendants' 'soldiers' 'lords' and others are often very important indeed in constructing meanings in performance.

The task of students and teacher in 'walking through' is to create their own stage-directions, as well as to examine those already indicated in the modern edition used as the basis for the work.

Discography

The position regarding the copyright of recorded material is complex. It is currently (1989) undergoing revision. As far as I am aware teachers may use recorded material in the classroom as part of their teaching provided there is no public performance resulting from it.

In my work I use music a great deal. It is invaluable in helping to create a good working atmosphere particularly when starting practical sessions; it is also very useful in helping to create and sustain an appropriate mood when working with spoken text. Music and songs from the Elizabethan/Jacobean period are now widely available on record and tape and these not only contribute to the sense of theatricality you can generate, but also give another insight for the student into the age and culture that generated the plays themselves. Also the BBC have issued a vast collection of weird and wonderful sound effects available on both disc and tape. At the end of the Discography I refer you to specific BBC recordings used in the practical exercises in Chapters 2 (p. 30) and 3 (p. 67).

I have divided the Discography into two sections. The first is of contemporary composers whose work I have used regularly in my own teaching. The second section deals with recordings by contemporary artists of music of Shakespeare's time. Needless to say, the selection of work in the latter is by no means representative; it simply reflects, as does the selection of contemporary work, pieces which I like and which the people I have taught have also liked and found helpful. One of the more enjoyable features of the preparation required for practical sessions is the time spent listening to music and thinking about how it might be used to enhance a particular exercise.

Contemporary music

Bhundu Boys

True Jit, WEA Cat No. WX 129 (disc and tape).
Tsvimbo-Dze-Moto, Discafrique Cat No. AFRI ZZ03.

Jarre, Jean Michel

Oxygene, Polydor Cat No. 2310 555 (disc) 3100 398 (tape).

Equinoxe, Polydor Cat No. POLD 5007 (disc) POLD 5007 (tape).
Magnetic Fields, Polydor Cat No. POLS 1033 (disc) POLSC 1033 (tape).
The Essential Jean Michel Jarre, Polydor, Cat No. PROLP 3 (disc).

Tangerine Dream

Dream Sequence, Virgin Records, Cat No. TDLP 1 (disc) TDC 1 (tape).
Flashpoint, Heavy Metal Worldwide, FM Revolver Records, Cat No. HMI MP 29 (disc) HMI MC 29 (tape).
The Tangerine Dream Collection, Castle Communications Records, Cat No. CCSLP 161 (disc; two) CCSMC 161-1/2 (tape: two).

Vangelis

Best of Vangelis, RCA Cat No. PL 70011 (disc) PK 70011 (tape).
Invisible Connections, DGG (Polydor) Cat No. 415 196 1 (disc) 415 196 4 (tape)
Heaven and Hell, RCA Cat No. NL 71148 (Disc) NK 71148 (tape).

Period music

Some of these recordings are no longer available, and some are available only on record. However, your local music library should be able to obtain them, and that will give you an idea of the kind of music I have used successfully. Although it is time consuming, trying to match text and sound is interesting and fun. Almost any of the current recordings of early music on tape and disc are potential sources of excellent material.

L'age D'Or Du Madrigal, The Deller Consort, Harmonia Mundi, Cat No. HMD 204.
Elizabethan and Jacobean Madrigals, The Scholars, Enigma Records, Cat No. VAR 1017.
English Madrigals, (2 records) Pro Cantione Antiqua, Oxford University Press, Cat No. OUP 151/2.
I love, alas: Elizabethan life in music song and poetry, Purcell Consort of Voices, Argo Records, Cat No. ZRG 652.
Lute Songs, Peter Pears and Julian Bream, Decca, Cat No. SA 7.
Portrait of Emma Kirkby, L'Oiseau-Lyre, Cat No. DSLO 607.
Elizabethan Heritage: Madrigals, Songs, and Harpsicord Pieces, The Madrigal Singers and the English Consort of Viols, Saga Records, Cat No. 5347.
The Triumph of Oriana, Purcell Chorus, London Cornet and Sackbut Ensemble, Elizabethan Consort of Viols, Argo Records, Cat No. ZRG 643.
Music to Entertain Elizabeth I, Purcell Chorus, Elizabethan Consort of Viols, Argo Records, Cat No. 2K 25.

Two Renaissance Dance Bands, the Early Music Consort of London, The Morley Consort, EMI, Cat No. HQS 1249. This record is particularly useful for music to dance to, and also for providing an appropriately 'formal' atmosphere in exercises requiring elaborate ritualised displays.

Non Stop Dancing 1600, Ulsamer Colleqium et al, Privilege Records, Cat No. 2538 348.

Renaissance Suite, David Munrow and the Early Music Consort of London, EMI, Cat No. HQS 1415.

Popular Music from the time of Queen Elizabeth I, The Camerata of London, Saga, Cat No. 5447. This record contains a wonderful recording by Glenda Simpson of two songs that I use a lot in my teaching: *Fortune my Foe* (Anon) and *Three Ravens* (Anon)

Four Last Songs, Richard Strauss, sung by Jessye Norman, Phillips, Cat No. 7337 322 (tape).

I refer in Chapter 2 to an exercise in which I suggest using the *Four Last Songs* of Richard Strauss. They are available in many different recordings but I particularly enjoy that by Jessye Norman. In a session at Cambridge, for the Shakespeare and Schools project, I used these songs in an exercise involving the Teacher Associates speaking chorically the song from *Cymbeline* 'Fear no more the heat o' th' sun,' (IV.2 258-281).

Sound effects

I found a recording of an owl hooting (*Macbeth,* Chapter 3) on *BBC Sound Effects No. 6,* BBC Records Cat No. 106M. Thunder, lightning and rain (*Macbeth,* Chapter 3) is on *BBC Sound Effects No. 7,* Cat No. RED 1135. There is a recording of 'men rioting' (*Julius Caesar,* Chapter 3) on *BBC Sound Effects No. 2,* Cat No. RED 76M.

Bibliography

Quotations from *Hamlet, Macbeth, Julius Caesar, Romeo and Juliet,* and *A Midsummer Night's Dream* are taken from the Oxford School Shakespeare series, edited by Roma Gill.

1 Rites of Transition

There are enough good ideas for appropriate theatre games and exercises in the list below that should keep you going for a long time.

Theatre Games, Clive Barker, Methuen, 1985.
Playing the Game, Christine Poulter, Macmillan, 1987.
  This is a particularly useful book for someone unused to practical drama. It contains lots of terrific material.
100 + Ideas for Drama, Anna Sher and Charles Verrall, Heinemann Educational, 1975.
Another 100 + Ideas for Drama, Anna Sher and Charles Verrall, Heinemann Educational, 1987

There are also two other titles that you may find useful as they contain some excellent practical exercises for the body and the voice. Although designed for professional actors, I have used many exercises from them in my own 'rites of transition' and young people should not find them too difficult.

Voice and the Actor, Cicely Berry, Harrap, 1973.
The Actor and His Body, Litz Pisk, Harrap, 1975.

2 and 3 Speaking the Text and Practical Approaches to: *Hamlet, Macbeth and Julius Caesar*

There are a number of books that have a bearing on a practical approach to teaching Shakespeare. I found the following helpful:

Teaching Shakespeare: Essays on approaches to Shakespeare in Schools and Colleges, Ed. Richard Adams, Robert Royce, 1985.
The Actor and His Text, Cicely Berry, Harrap, 1987.

Scripted Drama: A Practical Guide to Teaching Techniques, Alan England,
   Cambridge University Press, 1981. Contains a lot of material on teaching
   Shakespeare.
From Page to Stage, Bernadette Fitzgerald, published by Avon County Council
   as part of the SCDC National Writing Project, and available from: Oracy
   Project, Locking Primary School, Meadow Drive, Locking, Weston-super-
   Mare BS24 8BB.
Teaching Shakespeare, Veronica O'Brien, Edward Arnold, 1982.
English through Drama: a way of teaching, Christopher Parry, Cambridge
   University Press, 1972. See especially chapter 6 on teaching Shakespeare to
   12 year old boys.
London Drama Volume 6, Number 8, Summer 1983 was taken up with issues
   connected with teaching Shakespeare. Contributions from actors, directors
   and teachers.

4 Walking Through

There is a whole library of books dealing with performance orientated modes
of study. I have insufficient space to mention more than a few.

Players of Shakespeare, Ed. Philip Brockbank, Cambridge University Press,
   1985. (A collection of twelve essays by actors on acting Shakespeare.)
Elizabethan Popular Theatre, Michael Hattaway, Routledge & Kegan Paul, 1982.
Shakespeare: Text Into Performance, Peter Reynolds, Penguin Books, 1991.
   (Contains lots of examples of the page-to-stage process drawn from
   Shakespeare.)
Clamorous Voices: Shakespeare's Women Today, Ed. Carol Rutter, The Women's
   Press, 1988. (A stimulating collection of interviews with Sinead Cusack,
   Juliet Stevenson et. al. on what it's like to play some of the major female
   roles in Shakespeare.)
The Dramatic Experience: A Guide to the Reading of Plays, J. L. Styan,
   Cambridge University Press, 1965.
Players of Shakespeare 2, Eds. Russell Jackson and Robert Smallwood,
   Cambridge University Press, 1988.

Books about original playing conditions in the Elizabethan public theatre.

The Shakespearean Stage 1574–1642, Andrew Gurr, Cambridge University
   Press, 1982.
Shakespeare's Theatre, Peter Thomson, Routledge & Kegan Paul, 1983.

Other titles

Shakespeare Stories, Leon Garfield, Gollancz, 1988.
Five Tales from Shakespeare, Bernard Miles, Hamlyn, 1988.

Visual Material

Paintings

There are obviously vast numbers of these scattered about art galleries round the world. What follows is a selection of largely nineteenth century paintings mostly inspired by Shakespeare's *A Midsummer Night's Dream*. All of them can be seen in galleries in the UK, most of them in the Tate Gallery, London, who, on request, and for a small fee, will send you a reproduction for use in your teaching.

William Blake (1757-1827), *Oberon, Titania and Puck with Faeries dancing* (1785), Pencil and watercolour. Tate Gallery.

Henry Fuseli (1721-1825), *Titania and Bottom* (c. 1780-90), Oils. Tate Gallery.

Francis Danby (1793-1861), *Scene from 'A Midsummer Night's Dream'* (1832), Watercolour. Oldham Art Gallery and Museum.

David Scott (1806-49), *Puck fleeing before the dawn* (1837), Oils. National Gallery of Scotland.

Richard Dadd (1817-96), *The Fairy Feller's Master-Stroke* (1855-64), Oils. Tate Gallery.

Robert Huskisson (1820-61), *The Midsummer Night's Faeries* (c.1847), Oils. Tate Gallery.

Sir Joseph Noel Paton (1821-1901), *The quarrel of Oberon and Titania* (1849), Oils; *The reconciliation of Oberon and Titania* (1847), Oils. National Gallery of Scotland.

John Simmons (1823-76), *Titania* (1866), Watercolour. Bristol City Art Gallery.

Shakespeare on Video

Occasionally during this book I urge teachers to use video recordings of Shakespeare's plays to complement their practical teaching. There is an ever increasing library of recordings of Shakespeare that makes available classics like Olivier's 1948 film of *Hamlet*, to Kenneth Branagh's 1989 film of *Henry V*. Many plays from the *BBC/TIME Life Shakespeare Series* are now on sale (including *Macbeth*, *Hamlet* and *King Lear*). Obviously *all* this material is of varying quality, but it does represent a useful teaching resource. Those teachers who already use video, and those who want to make better use of it, might find the following titles of some use.

Filming Shakespeare's Plays, Anthony Davies, Cambridge University Press, 1988. (Includes a useful and interesting analysis of all Olivier's film versions.)
Focus on Shakespearean Films, Ed. Charles W. Eckert, Prentice-Hall, New Jersey, U.S.A. 1972
Shakespeare, cinema and society, John Collick, Manchester University Press, 1989.
'Shakespeare on the Screen: A Selective Filmography', Graham Holderness and Christopher McCullough, in *Shakespeare Survey* 39, 1987.
Shakespeare on Film, Jack J. Jorgens, Indiana University Press, U.S.A. 1977.
Shakespeare and the Film, Roger Manvell, J. M. Dent, 1971.
'Unlocking the Box: Shakespeare on Film and Video', Peter Reynolds, in *Shakespeare and the Changing Curriculum*, Eds. Lesley Ayers and Nigel Wheale, Routledge, 1991.

Teachers contemplating using video in the classroom would find their knowledge of how the medium operates enhanced by looking at:

Reading Television, John Fisk and John Hartley, Methuen, 1978.
Television Drama: An Introduction, David Self, Macmillan, 1984.

For a small sum (£5.00 members, £9.50 non-members in 1990) teachers can obtain a useful booklet listing all currently available video/film material on Shakespeare from: The British Universities Film Council, 55 Greek Street, London W1.

Index